The Era of Reconstruction

1865–1877

THE ERA OF RECONSTRUCTION, 1865-1877

by Kenneth M. Stampp

Professor of American History,
University of California at Berkeley

Vintage Books
A Division of Random House
New York

First Vintage Books Edition, September, 1967

© Copyright, 1965, by Kenneth M. Stampp

All rights reserved under International and Pan-American Copyright Conventions. Distributed in Canada by Random House of Canada Limited, Toronto.

*Reprinted by arrangement with
Alfred A. Knopf, Inc.*

Chapter Three, an expanded version of the author's inaugural lecture as Harmsworth Professor of American History, Oxford University, in 1962, was published by the Clarendon Press, Oxford, under the title *Andrew Johnson and the Failure of the Agrarian Dream.*

Manufactured in the United States of America

VINTAGE BOOKS
are published by
Alfred A. Knopf, Inc. and *Random House, Inc.*

For Isabel

FOREWORD

After the American Civil War the eleven states that had formed the southern Confederacy somehow had to be restored to their positions in the federal Union. President Lincoln, President Johnson, and Congress all tried their hands at providing them with loyal governments and at defining the role that the emancipated Negroes should play. What the presidential and congressional plans implied, why Congress eventually prevailed, how the South fared during the brief interlude of "radical" rule, and how this epoch affected the subsequent development of the South are the central topics of this book.

A half century ago, most historians were extremely critical of the reconstruction measures that congressional Republicans forced upon the defeated South. They used terms such as "military despotism," "federal tyranny," "Negro rule," and "Africanization" to describe what white Southerners were forced to endure. More recently, the leaders of the resistance to civil rights legislation and racial integration have evoked the hobgoblins of reconstruction to advance their cause. Yet, during the past generation, historians have written numerous books and articles which demonstrate that many of the popular notions about the era of reconstruction are distorted or untrue.

The legend nevertheless lives on. For example, two liberally inclined northern newspaper columnists, James Reston and Drew Pearson, still accept its basic tenets. According to Reston, the Republican policy of reconstruction was "vicious"; according to Pearson, "Negro extremists," by their "excesses" and "highhanded methods," lost the support of their white friends and "set back Negro progress by half a century."

This brief political history of reconstruction is an attempt to give more general currency to the findings of scholars during the past few decades. My own synthesis evolved gradually as I accumulated material on reconstruction for lectures to college students; it took its present form when I selected this topic for my Commonwealth Fund Lectures at the University of London in 1960. Since then I have expanded and rewritten the lectures to make them more suitable for publication. Except when I have quoted from recent historical works, I have not included footnote citations to sources. However, my bibliographical essay will refer readers to the books and articles that I have found most useful.

I am grateful to Richard N. Current, Lawrence W. Levine, Leon F. Litwack, and Charles G. Sellers, Jr., for their critical readings of my manuscript. Needless to say, responsibility for its remaining shortcomings is mine alone. I am also indebted to the Institute of Social Sciences of the University of California for providing funds for research assistance and typing.

KENNETH M. STAMPP

Berkeley, California

[ix]

CONTENTS

The Era of Reconstruction

1865–1877

CHAPTER ONE

The Tragic Legend of Reconstruction

In much serious history, as well as in a durable popular legend, two American epochs—the Civil War and the reconstruction that followed—bear an odd relationship to one another. The Civil War, though admittedly a tragedy, is nevertheless often described as a glorious time of gallantry, noble self-sacrifice, and high idealism. Even historians who have considered the war "needless" and have condemned the politicians of the 1850's for blundering into it, once they passed the firing on Fort Sumter, have usually written with reverence about Civil War heroes—the martyred Lincoln, the Christlike Lee, the intrepid Stonewall Jackson, and many others in this galaxy of demigods.

Few, of course, are so innocent as not to know that the Civil War had its seamy side. One can hardly ignore the political opportunism, the graft and profiteering in the filling of war contracts, the military blundering and needless loss of lives, the horrors of army hospitals and prison camps, and the ugly depths as well as the nobility of human nature that the war exposed with a fine impartiality. These things cannot be ignored, but they can be, and frequently are, dismissed as something alien to the essence of the war years. What was real and fundamental was the idealism and the nobility of the two contending forces: the Yankees struggling to save the Union, dying to make men free; the Confederates fighting for great constitutional principles, defending their homes from invasion. Here, indeed, is one of the secrets of the spell the Civil War has cast: it involved high-minded Americans on both sides, and there was glory enough to go around. This, in fact, is the supreme synthesis of Civil War historiography and the great balm that has healed the nation's wounds: Yankees and Confederates alike fought bravely for what they believed to be just causes. There were few villains in the drama.

But when the historian reaches the year 1865, he must take leave of the war and turn to another epoch, reconstruction, when the task was, in Lincoln's words, "to bind up the nation's wounds" and "to do all which may achieve and cherish a just and lasting peace." How, until recently, reconstruction was portrayed in both history and legend, how sharply it was believed to contrast with the years of the Civil War, is evident in the terms that were used to identify it. Various historians have called this phase of American history "The Tragic Era," "The Dreadful Decade," "The Age of Hate," and "The Blackout of Honest Government." Reconstruction represented the ultimate shame of the American people—as one historian phrased it, "the nadir of national disgrace." It was the epoch that most Americans wanted to forget.

Claude Bowers, who divided his time between politics and history, has been the chief disseminator of the traditional picture of reconstruction, for his book, *The Tragic Era,* published in 1929, has attracted more readers than any other dealing with this period. For Bowers reconstruction was a time of almost unrelieved sordidness in public and private life; whole regiments of villains march through his pages: the corrupt politicians who dominated

4

I: *The Tragic Legend of Reconstruction*

the administration of Ulysses S. Grant; the crafty, scheming northern carpetbaggers who invaded the South after the war for political and economic plunder; the degraded and depraved southern scalawags who betrayed their own people and collaborated with the enemy; and the ignorant, barbarous, sensual Negroes who threatened to Africanize the South and destroy its Caucasian civilization.

Most of Bowers's key generalizations can be found in his preface. The years of reconstruction, he wrote, "were years of revolutionary turmoil, with the elemental passions predominant. . . . The prevailing note was one of tragedy. . . . Never have American public men in responsible positions, directing the destiny of the nation, been so brutal, hypocritical, and corrupt. The constitution was treated as a doormat on which politicians and army officers wiped their feet after wading in the muck. . . . The southern people literally were put to the torture . . . [by] rugged conspirators . . . [who] assumed the pose of philanthropists and patriots." The popularity of Bowers's book stems in part from the simplicity of his characters. None are etched in shades of gray; none are confronted with complex moral decisions. Like characters in a Victorian romance, the Republican leaders of the reconstruction era were evil through and through, and the helpless, innocent white men of the South were totally noble and pure.

If Bowers's prose is more vivid and his anger more intense, his general interpretation of reconstruction is only a slight exaggeration of a point of view shared by most serious American historians from the late nineteenth century until very recently. Writing in the 1890's, James Ford Rhodes, author of a multi-volumed history of the United States since the Compromise of 1850, branded the Republican scheme of reconstruction as "repressive" and "uncivilized," one that "pandered to the ignorant negroes,

5

the knavish white natives and the vulturous adventurers who flocked from the North." About the same time Professor John W. Burgess, of Columbia University, called reconstruction the "most soul-sickening spectacle that Americans had ever been called upon to behold."[1] Early in the twentieth century Professor William A. Dunning, also of Columbia University, and a group of talented graduate students wrote a series of monographs that presented a crushing indictment of the Republican reconstruction program in the South—a series that made a deep and lasting impression on American historians. In the 1930's, Professor James G. Randall, of the University of Illinois, still writing in the spirit of the Dunningites, described the reconstruction era "as a time of party abuse, of corruption, of vindictive bigotry." "To use a modern phrase," wrote Randall, "government under Radical Republican rule in the South had become a kind of 'racket.' " As late as 1947, Professor E. Merton Coulter, of the University of Georgia, reminded critics of the traditional interpretation that no "amount of revision can write away the grievous mistakes made in this abnormal period of American history."[2] Thus, from Rhodes and Burgess and Dunning to Randall and Coulter the central emphasis of most historical writing about reconstruction has been upon sordid motives and human depravity. Somehow, during the summer of 1865, the nobility and idealism of the war years had died.

A synopsis of the Dunning School's version of recon-

---

[1] James Ford Rhodes: *History of the United States from the Compromise of 1850* . . . , 7 vols. (New York, 1893–1906), Vol. VII, p. 168; John W. Burgess: *Reconstruction and the Constitution* (New York, 1902) , p. 263.

[2] James G. Randall: *Civil War and Reconstruction* (Boston, 1937) , pp. 689, 852; E. Merton Coulter: *The South during Reconstruction, 1865–1877* (Baton Rouge, 1947), p. xi.

struction would run something like this: Abraham Lincoln, while the Civil War was still in progress, turned his thoughts to the great problem of reconciliation; and, "with malice toward none and charity for all," this gentle and compassionate man devised a plan that would restore the South to the Union with minimum humiliation and maximum speed. But there had already emerged in Congress a faction of radical Republicans, sometimes called Jacobins or Vindictives, who sought to defeat Lincoln's generous program. Motivated by hatred of the South, by selfish political ambitions, and by crass economic interests, the radicals tried to make the process of reconstruction as humiliating, as difficult, and as prolonged as they possibly could. Until Lincoln's tragic death, they poured their scorn upon him—and then used his coffin as a political stump to arouse the passions of the northern electorate.

The second chapter of the Dunning version begins with Andrew Johnson's succession to the presidency. Johnson, the old Jacksonian Unionist from Tennessee, took advantage of the adjournment of Congress to put Lincoln's mild plan of reconstruction into operation, and it was a striking success. In the summer and fall of 1865, Southerners organized loyal state governments, showed a willingness to deal fairly with their former slaves, and in general accepted the outcome of the Civil War in good faith. In December, when Congress assembled, President Johnson reported that the process of reconstruction was nearly completed and that the old Union had been restored. But the radicals unfortunately had their own sinister purposes: they repudiated the governments Johnson had established in the South, refused to seat southern Senators and Representatives, and then directed their fury against the new President. After a year of bitter controversy and political stalemate, the radicals, resorting to shamefully demagogic tactics, won an overwhelming victory in the congressional elections of 1866.

Now, the third chapter and the final tragedy. Riding roughshod over presidential vetoes and federal courts, the radicals put the South under military occupation, gave the ballot to Negroes, and formed new southern state governments dominated by base and corrupt men, black and white. Not satisfied with reducing the South to political slavery and financial bankruptcy, the radicals even laid their obscene hands on the pure fabric of the federal Constitution. They impeached President Johnson and came within one vote of removing him from office, though they had no legal grounds for such action. Next, they elected Ulysses S. Grant President, and during his two administrations they indulged in such an orgy of corruption and so prostituted the civil service as to make Grantism an enduring symbol of political immorality.

The last chapter is the story of ultimate redemption. Decent southern white Democrats, their patience exhausted, organized to drive the Negroes, carpetbaggers, and scalawags from power, peacefully if possible, forcefully if necessary. One by one the southern states were redeemed, honesty and virtue triumphed, and the South's natural leaders returned to power. In the spring of 1877, the Tragic Era finally came to an end when President Hayes withdrew the federal troops from the South and restored home rule. But the legacy of radical reconstruction remained in the form of a solidly Democratic South and embittered relations between the races.

This point of view was rarely challenged until the 1930's, when a small group of revisionist historians began to give new life and a new direction to the study of reconstruction. The revisionists are a curious lot who sometimes quarrel with each other as much as they quarrel with the disciples of Dunning. At various times they have counted in their ranks Marxists of various degrees of orthodoxy, Negroes seeking historical vindication, skeptical white Southerners, and latter-day northern abolitionists. But among them are numerous scholars who have the wisdom to know that the history of an age is seldom simple and clear-cut, seldom without its tragic aspects, seldom without its redeeming virtues.

Few revisionists would claim that the Dunning interpretation of reconstruction is a pure fabrication. They recognize the shabby aspects of this era: the corruption was real, the failures obvious, the tragedy undeniable. Grant is not their idea of a model President, nor were the southern carpetbag governments worthy of their unqualified praise. They understand that the radical Republicans were not all selfless patriots, and that southern white men were not all Negro-hating rebels. In short, they have not turned history on its head, but rather, they recognize that much of what Dunning's disciples have said about reconstruction is true.

Revisionists, however, have discovered that the Dunningites overlooked a great deal, and they doubt that nobility and idealism suddenly died in 1865. They are neither surprised nor disillusioned to find that the Civil War, for all its nobility, revealed some of the ugliness of human nature as well. And they approach reconstruction with the confident expectation that here, too, every facet of human nature will be exposed. They are not satisfied with the two-dimensional characters that Dunning's disciples have painted.

What is perhaps most puzzling in the legend of reconstruction is the notion that the white people of the South were treated with unprecedented brutality, that their conquerors, in Bowers's colorful phrase, literally put them to

9

the torture. How, in fact, *were* they treated after the failure of their rebellion against the authority of the federal government? The great mass of ordinary Southerners who voluntarily took up arms, or in other ways supported the Confederacy, were required simply to take an oath of allegiance to obtain pardon and to regain their right to vote and hold public office. But what of the Confederate leaders—the men who held high civil offices, often after resigning similar federal offices; the military leaders who had graduated from West Point and had resigned commissions in the United States Army to take commissions in the Confederate Army? Were there mass arrests, indictments for treason or conspiracy, trials and convictions, executions or imprisonments? Nothing of the sort. Officers of the Confederate Army were paroled and sent home with their men. After surrendering at Appomattox, General Lee bid farewell to his troops and rode home to live his remaining years undisturbed. Only one officer, a Captain Henry Wirtz, was arrested; and he was tried, convicted, and executed, not for treason or conspiracy, but for "war crimes." Wirtz's alleged offense, for which the evidence was rather flimsy, was the mistreatment of prisoners of war in the military prison at Andersonville, Georgia.

Of the Confederate civil officers, a handful were arrested at the close of the war, and there was talk for a time of trying a few for treason. But none, actually, was ever brought to trial, and all but Jefferson Davis were released within a few months. The former Confederate President was held in prison for nearly two years, but in 1867 he too was released. With a few exceptions, even the property of Confederate leaders was untouched, save, of course, for the emancipation of their slaves. Indeed, the only penalty imposed on most Confederate leaders was a temporary political disability provided in the Fourteenth Amendment. But in 1872 Congress pardoned all but a handful of Southerners; and soon former Confederate civil and military leaders were serving as state governors, as members of Congress, and even as Cabinet advisers of Presidents.

What, then, constituted the alleged brutality that white Southerners endured? First, the freeing of their slaves; second, the brief incarceration of a few Confederate leaders; third, a political disability imposed for a few years on most Confederate leaders; fourth, a relatively weak military occupation terminated in 1877; and, last, an attempt to extend the rights and privileges of citizenship to southern Negroes. Mistakes there were in the implementation of these measures—some of them serious—but brutality almost none. In fact, it can be said that rarely in history have the participants in an unsuccessful rebellion endured penalties as mild as those Congress imposed upon the people of the South, and particularly upon their leaders. After four years of bitter struggle costing hundreds of thousands of lives, the generosity of the federal government's terms was quite remarkable.

If northern brutality is a myth, the scandals of the Grant administration and the peculations of some of the southern reconstruction governments are sordid facts. Yet even here the Dunningites are guilty of distortion by exaggeration, by a lack of perspective, by superficial analysis, and by overemphasis. They make corruption a central theme of their narratives, but they overlook constructive accomplishments. They give insufficient attention to the men who transcended the greed of an age when, to be sure, self-serving politicians and irresponsible entrepreneurs were all too plentiful. Among these men were the humanitarians who organized Freedmen's Aid Societies to help

four million southern Negroes make the difficult transition from slavery to freedom, and the missionaries and
teachers who went into the South on slender budgets to
build churches and schools for the freedmen. Under their
auspices the Negroes first began to learn the responsibilities and obligations of freedom. Thus the training of
Negroes for citizenship had its successful beginnings in
the years of reconstruction.

In the nineteenth century most white Americans, North
and South, had reservations about the Negro's poten-
tialities—doubted that he had the innate intellectual
capacity and moral fiber of the white man and assumed
that after emancipation he would be relegated to an
inferior caste. But some of the radical Republicans refused
to believe that the Negroes were innately inferior and
hoped passionately that they would confound their critics.
The radicals then had little empirical evidence and no
scientific evidence to support their belief—nothing, in
fact, but faith. Their faith was derived mostly from their
religion: all men, they said, are the sons of Adam and
equal in the sight of God. And if Negroes are equal to
white men in the sight of God, it is morally wrong for
white men to withhold from Negroes the liberties and
rights that white men enjoy. Here, surely, was a projection
into the reconstruction era of the idealism of the abolitionist crusade and of the Civil War.

Radical idealism was in part responsible for two of the
most momentous enactments of the reconstruction years:
the Fourteenth Amendment to the federal Constitution
which gave Negroes citizenship and promised them equal
protection of the laws, and the Fifteenth Amendment
which\ gave them the right to vote. The fact that these
amendments could not have been adopted under any
other circumstances, or at any other time, before or since,

may suggest the crucial importance of the reconstruction era in American history. Indeed, without radical reconstruction, it would be impossible to this day for the federal government to protect Negroes from legal and political discrimination.

If all of this is true, or even part of it, why was the Dunning legend born, and why has it been so durable? Southerners, of course, have contributed much to the legend of reconstruction, but most Northerners have found the legend quite acceptable. Many of the historians who helped to create it were Northerners, among them James Ford Rhodes, William A. Dunning, Claude Bowers, and James G. Randall. Thus the legend cannot be explained simply in terms of a southern literary or historiographical conspiracy, satisfying as the legend has been to most white Southerners. What we need to know is why it also satisfies Northerners—how it became part of the intellectual baggage of so many northern historians. Why, in short, was there for so many years a kind of national, or inter-sectional, consensus that the Civil War was America's glory and reconstruction her disgrace?

The Civil War won its place in the hearts of the American people because, by the end of the nineteenth century, Northerners were willing to concede that Southerners had fought bravely for a cause that they believed to be just; whereas Southerners, with few exceptions, were willing to concede that the outcome of the war was probably best for all concerned. In an era of intense nationalism, both Northerners and Southerners agreed that the preservation of the federal Union was essential to the future power of the American people. Southerners could even say now that the abolition of slavery was one of the war's great blessings—not so much, they insisted, because slavery was an injustice to the Negroes but because it was a grievous burden upon the whites. By 1886, Henry W. Grady, the great Georgia editor and spokesman for a New South, could confess to a New York audience: "I am glad that the omniscient God held the balance of battle in His Almighty hand, and that human slavery was swept forever from American soil—the American Union saved from the wreck of war." Soon Union and Confederate veterans were holding joint reunions, exchanging anecdotes, and sharing their sentimental memories of those glorious war years. The Civil War thus took its position in the center of American folk mythology.

That the reconstruction era elicits neither pride nor sentimentality is due only in part to its moral delinquencies—remember, those of the Civil War years can be overlooked. It is also due to the white American's ambivalent attitude toward race and toward the steps that radical Republicans took to protect the Negroes. Southern white men accepted the Thirteenth Amendment to the Constitution, which abolished slavery, with a minimum of complaint, but they expected federal intervention to proceed no further than that. They assumed that the regulation of the freedmen would be left to the individual states; and clearly most of them intended to replace slavery with a caste system that would keep the Negroes perpetually subordinate to the whites. Negroes were to remain a dependent laboring class; they were to be governed by a separate code of laws; they were to play no active part in the South's political life; and they were to be segregated socially. When radical Republicans used federal power to interfere in these matters, the majority of southern white men formed a resistance movement to fight the radical-dominated state governments until they were overthrown, after which southern whites established a caste system in defiance of federal statutes and constitutional amendments. For many decades thereafter the federal government simply admitted defeat and acquiesced; but the South refused to forget or forgive those years of humiliation when Negroes came close to winning equality. In southern mythology, then, reconstruction was a horrid nightmare.

As for the majority of northern white men, it is hard to tell how deeply they were concerned about the welfare of the American Negro after the abolition of slavery. If one were to judge from the way they treated the small number of free Negroes who resided in the northern states, one might conclude that they were, at best, indifferent to the problem—and that a considerable number of them shared the racial attitudes of the South and preferred to keep Negroes in a subordinate caste. For a time after the Civil War the radical Republicans, who were always a minority group, persuaded the northern electorate that the ultimate purpose of southern white men was to rob the North of the fruits of victory and to re-establish slavery and that federal intervention was therefore essential. In this manner radicals won approval of, or acquiescence in, their program to give civil rights and the ballot to southern Negroes. Popular support for the radical program waned rapidly, however, and by the middle of the 1870's it had all but vanished. In 1875 a Republican politician confessed that northern voters were tired of the "worn-out cry of 'southern outrages,'" and they wished that "the 'nigger' the 'everlasting nigger' were in—Africa." As Northerners ceased to worry about the possibility of another southern rebellion, they became increasingly receptive to criticism of radical reconstruction.

The eventual disintegration of the radical phalanx,

15

those root-and-branch men who, for a time, seemed bent on engineering a sweeping reformation of southern society, was another important reason for the denigration of reconstruction in American historiography. To be sure, some of the radicals, especially those who had been abolitionists before the war, never lost faith in the Negro, and in the years after reconstruction they stood by him as he struggled to break the intellectual and psychological fetters he had brought with him out of slavery. Other radicals, however, lost interest in the cause—tired of reform and spent their declining years writing their memoirs. Still others retained their crusading zeal but became disenchanted with radical reconstruction and found other crusades more attractive: civil service reform, or tariff reform, or defense of the gold standard. In 1872 they repudiated Grant and joined the Liberal Republicans; in subsequent years they considered themselves to be political independents.

This latter group had been an important element in the original radical coalition. Most of them were respectable, middle-class people in comfortable economic circumstances, well educated and highly articulate, and acutely conscious of their obligation to perform disinterested public service. They had looked upon Senator Charles Sumner of Massachusetts as their political spokesman, and upon Edwin L. Godkin of the New York *Nation* as their editorial spokesman. Like most radicals they had believed that the Negro was what slavery had made him; give the Negro equal rights and he would be quickly transformed into an industrious and responsible citizen. With the radical reconstruction program fairly launched, they had looked forward to swift and dramatic results.

But reconstruction was not as orderly and the Negro's

progress was not nearly as swift and dramatic as these reformers had seemed to expect. The first signs of doubt came soon after the radicals won control of reconstruction policy, when the *Nation* warned the Negroes that the government had already done all it could for them. They were now, said the *Nation,* "on the dusty and rugged highway of competition"; henceforth "the removal of white prejudice against the Negro depends almost entirely on the Negro himself." By 1870 this bellwether of the reformers viewed with alarm the disorders and irregularities in the states governed by Negroes and carpetbaggers; by 1871 it proclaimed: "The experiment has totally failed. . . . We owe it to human nature to say that worse governments have seldom been seen in a civilized country." And three years later, looking at South Carolina, the *Nation* pronounced the ultimate epithet: "This is . . . socialism." Among the former radicals associated with the *Nation* in these years of tragic disillusionment were three prewar abolitionists: Edmund Quincy of Massachusetts, James Miller McKim of Pennsylvania, and the Reverend O. B. Frothingham of New York.

Finally, in 1890, many years after the reconstruction governments had collapsed, the *Nation,* still accurately reflecting the state of mind of the disenchanted reformers, made a full confession of its past errors. "There is," said the *Nation,* "a rapidly growing sympathy at the North with Southern perplexity over the negro problem. . . . Even those who were not shocked by the carpet-bag experiment . . . are beginning to 'view with alarm' the political prospect created by the increase of the negro population, and by the continued inability of southern society to absorb or assimilate them in any sense, physical, social, or political. . . . The sudden admission to the suffrage of a million of the recently emancipated slaves belonging to the least civilized race in the world . . . was a great leap in the dark, the ultimate consequences of which no man now living can foresee. No nation has ever done this, or anything like this for the benefit of aliens of any race or creed. Who or what is . . . [the Negro] that we should put the interests of the 55,000,000 whites on this continent in peril for his sake?" Editor Godkin answered his own question in a letter to another one-time radical: "I do not see . . . how the negro is ever to be worked into a system of government for which you and I would have much respect."

Actually, neither the obvious shortcomings of reconstruction nor an objective view of the Negro's progress in the years after emancipation can wholly explain the disillusionment of so many former radicals. Rather, their changed attitude toward the Negro and the hostile historical interpretation of reconstruction that won their favor were in part the product of social trends that severely affected the old American middle classes with whom most of them were identified. These trends had their origin in the industrial revolution; they were evident in the early nineteenth century but were enormously accelerated after the Civil War. Their institutional symbols were the giant manufacturing and railroad corporations.

In the new age of industrial enterprise there seemed to be no place for the old families with their genteel culture and strong traditions of disinterested public service. On the one hand, they were overshadowed by new and powerful industrial capitalists whose economic strength brought with it vast political influence. Legislative bodies became arenas in which the political vassals of oil, steel, and railroad barons struggled for special favors, while the interests of the public—and the old middle classes liked to think of themselves as *the public—* counted for nothing. On the other hand, they were threatened by the immigrants who came to America to work in the mines and mills and on the railroads—Italians, Slavs, and Jews from Poland and Russia. The immigrants crowded into the tenements of eastern cities, responded to the friendly overtures of urban political bosses, and used their ballots to evict the old middle-class families from power. Here was a threat to the traditional America that these families had loved—and dominated—to that once vigorous American nationality that was Protestant, Anglo-Saxon, and pure. Henry James commented bitterly about the people he met on Boston Common during a stroll one Sunday afternoon: "No sound of English, in a single instance escaped their lips; the greater number spoke a rude form of Italian, the others some outland dialect unknown to me. . . . The types and faces bore them out; the people before me were gross aliens to a man, and they were in serene and triumphant possession."

Soon the new immigrant groups had become the victims of cruel racial stereotypes. Taken collectively it would appear that they were, among other things, innately inferior to the Anglo-Saxons in their intellectual and physical traits, dirty and immoral in their habits, inclined toward criminality, receptive to dangerous political beliefs, and shiftless and irresponsible.

In due time, those who repeated these stereotypes awoke to the realization that what they were saying was not really very original—that, as a matter of fact, these generalizations were *precisely* the ones that southern white men had been making about Negroes for years. And, in their extremity, the old middle classes of the North looked with new understanding upon the problems of the beleaguered white men of the South. Perhaps all along

Southerners had understood the problem better than they. Here, then, was a crucial part of the intellectual climate in which the Dunning interpretation of reconstruction was written. It was written at a time when xenophobia had become almost a national disease, when the immigration restriction movement was getting into high gear, when numerous northern cities (among them Philadelphia and Chicago) were seriously considering the establishment of racially segregated schools, and when Negroes and immigrants were being lumped together in the category of unassimilable aliens.

Several other attitudes, prevalent in the late nineteenth century, encouraged an interpretation of reconstruction that condemned radical Republicans for meddling in southern race relations. The vogue of social Darwinism discouraged governmental intervention in behalf of Negroes as well as other underprivileged groups; it encouraged the belief that a solution to the race problem could only evolve slowly as the Negroes gradually improved themselves. A rising spirit of nationalism stimulated a desire for sectional reconciliation, and part of the price was a virtual abdication of federal responsibility for the protection of the Negro's civil and political rights. An outburst of imperialism manifested in the Spanish-American War and the annexation of the Hawaiian Islands, found one of its principal justifications in the notion that Anglo-Saxons were superior to other peoples, especially when it came to politics. In the words of Senator Albert J. Beveridge of Indiana: "God has not been preparing the English-speaking and Teutonic people for a thousand years for nothing but vain and idle self-admiration. No! He has made us the master organizers of the world to establish system where chaos reigns. . . . He has made us adepts in government that we may administer government among savages and senile peoples." What folly, then, to expect Italians and Slavs to behave like Anglo-Saxons—or to accept the sentimental doctrine that Negroes deserve to be given the same political rights as white men!

Finally, at this critical juncture, sociologists, anthropologists, and psychologists presented what they regarded as convincing evidence of innate racial traits—evidence indicating that Negroes were intellectually inferior to whites and had distinctive emotional characteristics. The social scientists thus supplied the racists of the late nineteenth and early twentieth centuries with something that ante-bellum pro-slavery writers had always lacked: a respectable scientific argument. When, in 1916, Madison Grant, an amateur cultural anthropologist, published *The Passing of the Great Race,* his racism was only a mild caricature of a point of view shared by numerous social scientists. Examining the history of the United States, Grant easily detected her tragic blunder:

> Race consciousness . . . in the United States, down to and including the Mexican War, seems to have been very strongly developed among native Americans, and it still remains in full vigor today in the South, where the presence of a large negro population forces this question upon the daily attention of the whites. . . . In New England, however . . . there appeared early in the last century a wave of sentimentalism, which at that time took up the cause of the negro, and in so doing apparently destroyed, to a large extent, pride and consciousness of race in the North. The agitation over slavery was inimical to the Nordic race, because it thrust aside all national opposition to the intrusion of hordes of immigrants of inferior racial value, and prevented the fixing of a definite American type. . . . The native American by the middle of the nineteenth century was

21

rapidly becoming a distinct type. . . . The Civil War, however, put a severe, perhaps fatal, check to the development and expansion of this splendid type, by destroying great numbers of the best breeding stock on both sides, and by breaking up the home ties of many more. If the war had not occurred these same men with their descendants would have populated the Western States instead of the racial nondescripts who are now flocking there.[3]

In this social atmosphere, armed with the knowledge of race that the social scientists had given them, historians exposed the folly of radical reconstruction. At the turn of the century, James Ford Rhodes, that intimate friend of New England Brahmins, gave his verdict on Negro suffrage—one that the Dunningites would soon develop into the central assumption, the controlling generalization, of the reconstruction legend. "No large policy in our country," concluded Rhodes, "has ever been so conspicuous a failure as that of forcing universal negro suffrage upon the South. . . . From the Republican policy came no real good to the negroes. Most of them developed no political capacity, and the few who raised themselves above the mass did not reach a high order of intelligence. . . . The negro's political activity is rarely of a nature to identify him with any movement on a high plane. . . . [He] has been politically a failure and he could not have been otherwise."[4]

In the course of time the social scientists drastically revised their notions about race, and in recent years most of them have been striving to destroy the errors in whose creation their predecessors played so crucial a part. As ideas

---

[3] Madison Grant: *The Passing of the Great Race* (New York, 1916), pp. 77–9.
[4] Rhodes: *History of the United States*, Vol VII, pp. 168–70.

I: *The Tragic Legend of Reconstruction*

about race have changed, historians have become increasingly critical of the Dunning interpretation of reconstruction. These changes, together with a great deal of painstaking research, have produced the revisionist writing of the past generation. It is dangerous, of course, for a historian to label himself as a revisionist, for his ultimate and inevitable fate is one day to have his own revisions revised.

But that has never discouraged revisionists, and we may hope that it never will, especially those who have been rewriting the history of the reconstruction era. One need not be disturbed about the romantic nonsense that still fills the minds of many Americans about their Civil War. This folklore is essentially harmless. But the legend of reconstruction is another matter. It has had serious consequences, because it has exerted a powerful influence upon the political behavior of many white men, North and South.

CHAPTER TWO

Abraham Lincoln: The Politics of a Practical Whig

The problem of political reconstruction arose, in theory at least, as soon as the Civil War began, because neither President Lincoln nor the Republican majority in Congress ever doubted that the South would ultimately be defeated. As early as July 4, 1861, Lincoln alluded to the subject in his message to a special session of Congress. "Lest there be some uneasiness," he said, "as to what is to be the course of the government towards the southern states, *after* the rebellion shall have been suppressed, the Executive deems it proper to say, it will be his purpose then, as ever, to be guided by the Constitution and the laws."

This statement was doubtless intended to assure Southerners that the war would not be followed by a Carthaginian peace. Actually, it meant virtually nothing, because there were almost no laws and there was little in the Constitution that had any relevance to the existing crisis. The crisis was, in fact, without a precedent. Since the birth of the Republic, one state or another had threatened, from time to time, to secede from the Union; but before 1860 no state had ever ventured beyond threats into action. When, finally, eleven states did adopt formal ordinances of secession, the northern Unionists and southern secessionists engaged in a fascinating but essentially irrelevant constitutional debate. The Constitution does not say that individual states may secede at their pleasure; neither does it say that they may not. Indeed, it says nothing one way or the other on the subject; and the secessionist argument, therefore, was based upon inference. In brief, the southern disunionists contended that the states were older than the Union; that in 1787 the states had created a voluntary Union, reserving to themselves the right to resume their independent status at will; and that the federal government was the mere creature of the states, without power to coerce them.

Lincoln, in his first inaugural address, summarized the Unionist position. He maintained that the Union was older than the states; that once in the Union, no state had the reserved power to get out; that each state had surrendered part of its sovereignty to the federal government; that in the exercise of its own powers the federal government operated directly on the people and not through the states. In his most persuasive argument, Lincoln virtually conceded that he could not use the actual language of the Constitution to support his position. "Perpetuity," he said, "is *implied* if not expressed, in the fundamental law of all national governments. It is safe to assert that no government proper, ever had a provision in its organic law for its own termination." And so, he concluded: "It follows from these views that no state upon its own mere motion, can lawfully get out of the Union,—that resolves and ordinances to that effect are legally void; and that acts of violence, within any state or states, are insurrectionary or revolutionary according to circumstances."[1]

---

[1] Damning Southerners as revolutionists was a little embarrassing to the northern grandsons of revolutionists, and it took some syllogistic ingenuity to prove that Southerners were specious revolutionists.

But Lincoln's case, like that of the secessionists, was only inferential. And since the Constitution says nothing about the right of secession, logically enough it says nothing about what the President or Congress may do if several states should try to secede. Lincoln, therefore, could only proceed from his assumption that ordinances of secession were legally void and that it was impossible for a state to separate itself from the federal Union. From this premise the obvious conclusion was that Southerners were actually engaged in a domestic insurrection, and on this subject the Constitution and the laws spoke with relative clarity. The Constitution authorizes Congress to provide for calling forth the militia to execute the laws and suppress insurrections, and several acts passed in earlier years enabled the President to make use of the militia in time of domestic crisis. The constitutional definition of treason, that is, that it consists of levying war against the United States, adhering to its enemies, or giving them aid and comfort, also seemed applicable to Southerners. So did a clause in the Constitution requiring the federal government to guarantee to every state a republican form of government, if one were to assume that governments dominated by slaveholders and rebels were not republican.

All of this gave the President and Congress what legal and constitutional grounds they had for action. Their problem was not to win an international war, not to bring the southern states back into the Union (for they had never been out), but to disperse bands of rebels and establish in the South loyal state governments. On this Lincoln was quite explicit when he first called out the militia. The call, he said in his proclamation of April 15, 1861, was to suppress combinations of disloyal citizens, to cause the laws to be duly executed, and to "redress wrongs already long enough endured." In practice, of course, the

war could not be waged as if the government were dealing with a domestic insurrection. Captured Confederates
were not treated as traitors but as prisoners of war, lest
the Confederate government retaliate against Union
prisoners. But whatever the practical inconsistencies, the
Lincoln administration would yield nothing in theory;
throughout the Civil War all of the official pronounce-
ments of the Executive Department referred to Southerners as "disloyal citizens," or "rebels," or "insurgents";
and after 1865 the official designation of this conflict was
"The War of the Rebellion."

Near the end of the war some of the radical Republicans in Congress, contemplating a more drastic program
of reconstruction than Lincoln's, began to find it useful to
their purposes to concede that the South actually had
separated from the Union and had established an independent government; the defeated South would then
lie prostrate before the North as a conquered province.
Lincoln's reply, in his last public speech before his death,
was that the friends of the Union were involving themselves in a pointless debate over what he called a "perni-
cious abstraction." The important fact, he insisted, was
that the southern states were "out of their proper practical
relation with the Union; and . . . the sole object of the
government . . . [was] again to get them into that proper
practical relation."

To Lincoln, restoring the old relationship between the
southern states and the Union was the essence of reconstruction. This task, he thought, belonged to the President, not to Congress. Lincoln was too wise a man ever to
say this bluntly to the legislative branch, but many times
he implied it as tactfully as he could, and always he acted
upon this assumption. He was commander in chief of the
armed forces; he had called out the militia; he had pro-

claimed martial law in the South; and he had the constitutional power to grant individual pardons or a general
amnesty to Southerners. It was his responsibility, therefore, to state the conditions of an amnesty, to decide when
loyal state governments had been re-established in the
South, and to fix the time for the revocation of martial
law.

Lincoln's radical Republican critics, however, believed
that the entire problem belonged to Congress. It was the
duty of Congress to guarantee to every state a republican
form of government; and Congress alone could determine
when the southern states would again be entitled to send
Senators and Representatives to Washington.

In the resulting conflict between the legislative and
executive branches, there was no way to decide whose
case was the stronger, for the Constitution is silent on the
point at issue. The most logical conclusion, however,
would seem to have been that reconstruction was a joint
responsibility of the President and Congress. The very
dimensions of the problem, as well as the lack of precedents, put Lincoln in an extremely vulnerable position
when he tried to go it alone. The real trouble, of course,
and the reason that this unfortunate controversy developed, was that the President and the radical Republicans in Congress were pressing conflicting plans of
reconstruction. No doubt, if their purposes had coincided,
the question of jurisdiction would never have arisen, and
President and Congress would have coexisted in perfect
harmony.

Lincoln, then, neither waited for Congress to act nor
consulted congressional leaders; instead, as soon as a substantial area of the South was under federal occupation,
he began to devise and implement a program of his own.
To understand the role that Lincoln played in the re-

construction of the South, to comprehend his ultimate goals, his program must be considered in part in political terms. Unfortunately Lincoln's admirers have often operated on the assumption that to call him a politician is somehow to degrade him; they reserve that label for his congressional critics.

This attitude toward Lincoln reflects a curious American attitude toward politics. As Richard N. Current has observed: "Among Americans the words *politics* and *politician* long have been terms of reproach. Politics generally means 'dirty' politics, whether the adjective is used or not. Politicians, then, are dirty politicians unless they happen to be statesmen, and in that case they are not politicians at all."[2] Lincoln himself contributed to this unpleasant image when, early in his career, he described politicians as "a set of men who have interests aside from the interests of the people, and who . . . are, taken as a class, at least one long step removed from honest men."

And yet Lincoln's own much-admired statesmanship was based on a solid foundation of political talent and experience. He ranked loyalty to party high among human virtues; he understood the techniques of party management; he knew when to concede and when to hold firm; and he had a most sensitive feeling for trends in public opinion. Lincoln was an ambitious man—his ambition, said his former law partner, "was a little engine that knew no rest"—and he thoroughly understood that public office does not seek the man, but the man seeks the office. Accordingly, Lincoln was, from his early manhood, openly available, unblushingly eager for any office to which he could win appointment or election. Early in 1860, when the greatest prize of all seemed within reach, he confessed

---

[2] Richard N. Current: *The Lincoln Nobody Knows* (New York, 1958), p. 187.

to a friend with disarming candor, "The taste *is* in my mouth a little." He won the prize, and his masterful performance during his years as President has rarely been equaled and never surpassed. Under the most trying circumstances he presided over a Cabinet of prima donnas, held together his loosely organized party, and repeatedly outmaneuvered a dangerously powerful opposition party. "If Abraham Lincoln was not a master politician," wrote one of his admiring contemporaries who knew the meaning of the word, "I am entirely ignorant of the qualities which make up such a character. . . . No man knew better . . . how to summon and dispose of political ability to attain great political ends."

This is the man, it has often been made to appear, who approached the problem of postwar reconstruction without giving a thought to the political consequences of his plans. It was his innate generosity, his inner tenderness, and nothing else, that impelled him to extend to the South his generous terms, while selfish, scheming politicians in Congress cried out for vengeance. Nothing could be farther from the truth; nothing could more distort the character of the man.

Lincoln *was*, to be sure, a generous and tender man, and these personal qualities affected his program for the South. But he was also the leader of the Republican party, and he was still a loyal party man. Without his party he would have been powerless; and an analysis of his reconstruction program must begin with these rather obvious facts in mind. When Lincoln was President, the Republican party had no existence in the southern states; yet the ultimate political consequence of reconstruction would be the representation of these states in Congress once more. They would send twenty-two Senators and sixty-three Representatives, and they would have eighty-five votes in the

Electoral College. This, of course, was bound to weaken the position of Lincoln's party, unless some way could be found to organize it in the South—a most delicate task, since the Republicans would be the instrument of southern defeat. Here, if anywhere, was a worthy test of Lincoln's political skill.

Lincoln, then, was a politician; but he was a special kind of politician, which introduces another important part of the background of his reconstruction program. During most of his active political life, Lincoln had not been a Republican but a Whig. He had joined the Whigs in the 1830's, when they had first organized in opposition to the Jacksonian Democrats, and he was still a loyal Whig in the early 1850's. Lincoln was not one of the organizers of the new Republican party; rather, he clung to the old party until there was no life left in it and only then abandoned his first political love. If he had a political hero, it was Henry Clay of Kentucky, the great Whig statesman; still in 1861 he spoke of Clay as the man "whom, during my whole political life, I have loved and revered as a teacher and leader." A member of Lincoln's cabinet observed that he "is of the Whig school, and that brings him naturally . . . to give his confidence to such advisers."

Lincoln's Whig background is relevant to a consideration of his reconstruction goals, because the Whig party had been a national organization with powerful support in the South. When he served a term in Congress during the 1840's, Lincoln worked amiably with numerous southern Whig leaders; and still in the 1850's he remained on friendly terms with several of them. When the Whig party collapsed, southern Whigs were in a quandary; for its successor, the Republican party, was a northern anti-slavery organization and of course unacceptable to them.

Some of the old southern Whigs drifted, with the utmost reluctance, into the Democratic party; others found shelter briefly in short-lived third-party movements. But it was clear that when the Civil War was over and the Union restored, at least forty per cent of the white voters in the southern states would be men without a party—in a state of political flux. Where they would go was still an open question, for the solid Democratic South had not yet emerged. To Lincoln, the Republican party was the true heir of the Whig tradition; and with the slavery issue removed, why should not these politically homeless Southerners find a refuge in his party? Lincoln most emphatically did not intend that the Republicans should remain permanently a sectional organization; nor would he surrender to the Democrats his one-time Whig allies in the South.

This was the political background of Lincoln's reconstruction plans. The geographical background is also significant, because it may help to explain his ideas about the future of the American Negro after the abolition of slavery. Lincoln was born in Kentucky, a slave state, from whence he moved to southern Illinois, a region settled largely by Southerners. When Illinois was admitted to statehood in 1818, it was only after a prolonged political struggle that slavery was finally prohibited. But from then until the Civil War the small free Negro population was given the status of an inferior caste. Illinois Negroes could not vote or hold public office; they could not attend the public schools; and eventually further Negro migration into the state was prohibited. Such were the racial attitudes to which Lincoln was exposed in his youth, attitudes which he was never quite able to transcend.

Still in 1858, during his famous debates with Stephen A. Douglas, Lincoln assured his listeners: "I am not, nor ever have been in favor of bringing about in any way the social and political equality of the white and black races,—that I am not nor ever have been in favor of making voters or jurors of negroes, nor of qualifying them to hold office, nor to intermarry with white people; and I will say in addition to this that there is a physical difference between the white and black races which I believe will forever forbid the two races living together on terms of social and political equality. And inasmuch as they cannot so live, while they do remain together there must be the position of superior and inferior, and I as much as any other man am in favor of having the superior position assigned to the white race." On no other platform, Lincoln well understood, could a politician successfully bid for the support of Illinois voters. But there was no hypocrisy in these statements, for they expressed *his* conviction as much as they did the convictions of those to whom he spoke.

By the 1850's, perhaps sooner, Lincoln had concluded that *slavery* nevertheless was a great moral evil, but an evil that afforded no easy remedy. "If all earthly power were given me," he said, "I should not know what to do, as to the existing institution. . . . [Shall we] free them all and keep them among us as underlings? Is it quite certain that this betters their condition? I think I would not hold one in slavery . . . yet the point is not clear enough for me to denounce other people upon. . . . [Shall we] free them and make them politically and socially our equals? My own feelings will not admit of this." Lincoln, as he repeatedly affirmed, was not an abolitionist in these prewar years; and he understood, moreover, that much of the northern popular opposition to slavery expansion into new states and territories arose from a dislike of the Negro as well as from a dislike of slavery.

Lincoln frequently expressed his personal disagreement with the principle of slavery. In 1854 he described its "monstrous injustice"; in 1858 he demanded that it be placed "where the public mind shall rest in the belief that it is in course of ultimate extinction"; in 1864 he affirmed that "if slavery is not wrong, nothing is wrong." He also made it clear that, though he did not believe in the equality of the races, he did believe that Negroes had rights. In a speech in Springfield, Illinois, in 1858, he conceded that the Declaration of Independence did not mean that all men are created equal in all respects; but it did mean that all men "are equal in their right to 'life, liberty and the pursuit of happiness.'" Moreover, "in the right to put into his mouth the bread that his own hands have earned . . . [the Negro] is the equal of every other man, white or black."

But Lincoln could discover no better solution to the problem of slavery than a chimerical scheme that numerous men had been toying with since the early nineteenth century. What eventually caught his fancy was a plan of gradual emancipation stretching over a half century or more, financial compensation to the owners, and colonization of the free Negroes beyond the boundaries of the United States. They might be sent back to Africa, or to South America, or to Central America, or to the islands of the Caribbean.

This scheme may have been part of Lincoln's heritage from Henry Clay, for Clay had long been an active supporter of the American Colonization Society. When Lincoln eulogized Clay at the time of his death in 1852, he praised him for his work in the colonization movement. What a "glorious consummation" of Clay's work it would be, said Lincoln, if America could free itself from "the dangerous presence of slavery; and, at the same time . . .

[restore] a captive people to their long-lost father-land." Lincoln returned to this theme many times, suggesting on one occasion that separation of the races was the only way to prevent the evil of racial amalgamation. "Such separation," he added, "if ever effected at all, must be effected by colonization."

As late as 1862, in the second year of the Civil War and of his presidency, Lincoln addressed a group of Negroes in this fashion: "You and we are different races. We have between us a broader difference than exists between almost any other two races. . . . [This] physical difference is a great disadvantage to us both, as I think your race suffers very greatly . . . by living among us, while ours suffers from your presence. In a word, we suffer on each side. . . . It is better for us both, therefore, to be separated." In his message to Congress that December, Lincoln publicly reaffirmed this view: "I cannot make it better known than it already is, that I strongly favor colonization." It would appear, then, that Lincoln approached the problem of reconstruction with three assumptions regarding the American Negro: (1) emancipation from slavery must be gradual; (2) colonization was the ideal solution to the race problem; and (3) colonization failing, the free Negro would have to accept an inferior status in American society.

In viewing this man as he planned for the postwar years, we now have seen Lincoln the consummate politician; Lincoln the everlasting Whig; and Lincoln the enemy of slavery if not quite the friend of the Negro. But no doubt Lincoln's character, especially his profound compassion and his tragic view of life, also helped to give shape to his reconstruction plans. During the war, Richard Hofstadter believes: "Lincoln was moved by the wounded and dying men, moved as no one in a place of power can afford to be. . . . For him it was impossible to drift into that habitual callousness of the sort of officialdom that sees men only as pawns to be shifted here and there and 'expended' at the will of others." Seldom has anyone exercised so much power and yet felt "so slightly the private corruption that goes with it."[3] Lincoln was too humble to judge the motives of Southerners or to assume that he was God's instrument for their chastisement; too much of a conservative to believe that it was even within his power to reform mankind or to change significantly existing social arrangements. For him, reconstruction was to be essentially a work of restoration, not innovation; it was the old Union—the Union as it was—that he hoped to rebuild.

Chastened as he was by the stern necessity to choose between life and death for others, feeling no malice toward and much charity for southern Confederates, Lincoln also betrayed a haunting sense of personal responsibility for the war that began in 1861. Between his election in November 1860 and his inauguration the following March, he had used all his influence to prevent the Republicans in Congress from offering to compromise with the South. "Stand firm," he told them. "The instant you . . . [compromise] they have us under again; all our labor is lost, and sooner or later must be done over. . . . Have none of it. The tug has to come, and better now than later." Rejecting compromise, rejecting also a peaceful dissolution of the federal Union, he faced the distasteful alternative of a resort to force, if southern secessionists were in earnest. It was his firm conviction that as President he would be obligated to execute the laws in all the states and to preserve the Union.

---

[3] Richard Hofstadter: *The American Political Tradition* (New York, 1948), pp. 134–5.

II: *Abraham Lincoln: The Politics of a Practical Whig*

Lincoln saw his duty, but to assume responsibility for the opening of hostilities was more than he could bear; and, accordingly, he repeatedly asserted that he would not be the aggressor if war should come. En route to Washington for his inauguration, he told a Philadelphia audience that he could see "in the present aspect of affairs . . . no need of bloodshed and war. . . . I am not in favor of such a course; and I may say in advance that there will be no bloodshed unless it is forced upon the government. The government will not use force, unless force is used against it." In his inaugural address, he warned Southerners that the issue of war was in their hands, not his. "You can have no conflict," he said, "without being yourselves the aggressors."

When, in April 1861, he decided the send a relief expedition to the federal garrison at Fort Sumter in Charleston harbor, he took pains to notify the governor of South Carolina in advance, and to assure the governor that he was only sending food to the starving garrison, not ammunition or reinforcements. When the Confederates opened fire on Fort Sumter, the vast majority of Northerners were convinced that this was an act of aggression and blamed the South for precipitating a war. But Lincoln was aware of the moral burden he had assumed—aware that to nearly every Southerner *he* was the aggressor in sending a naval expedition to Fort Sumter. For this sorely troubled man the presidency brought not the glory he had anticipated but, as he once confessed, only "ashes and blood." As he approached the problem of reconstruction, Lincoln still lacked that inward serenity enjoyed by those who never question their own values or doubt their moral rectitude; and it may well be that his effort to treat the South with the utmost generosity reflected, in part, his desire for personal absolution.

With these several political and personal predilections, Lincoln undertook one of the most challenging tasks ever to confront an American President: the repairing of the broken Union. In the re-establishment of loyal state governments he sought the co-operation of the minority of white Southerners who had remained faithful to the Union and of those who would voluntarily return to their former allegiance. Among these elements in the southern states he invariably found a preponderance of Whigs, for the Whigs as a group had tended to be less ardent for secession than the Democrats. This presented a fair chance that any new southern governments formed under Lincoln's direction would be Whig dominated, and the President had every reason to hope that the bridge from Whiggery to Republicanism would be an easy one. Before his death, Lincoln did make progress toward the formation of loyal governments in four southern states—Virginia, Tennessee, Louisiana, and Arkansas—and in each case the Whigs exerted considerable influence.

After the capture of New Orleans in the spring of 1862, Lincoln wrote to a Louisiana Unionist that the people of his state needed merely to establish a loyal state government. "The army," he promised, "will be withdrawn so soon as such state government can dispense with its presence; and the people of the state can then upon the old constitutional terms, govern themselves to their own liking." He would then favor the election of Congressmen, but the candidates must be "respectable citizens of Louisiana," not "a parcel of Northern men . . . elected . . . at the point of the bayonet." A year later, he was still urging the loyalists to go to work in Louisiana. All he asked for, he said, was "a tangible nucleus which the remainder of the state may rally around as fast as it can, and which I can at once recognize and sustain as the true state government." Late in the summer of 1863, he sent similar advice to Andrew Johnson, the military governor of Tennessee.

Eventually, on December 8, 1863, Lincoln issued a proclamation of amnesty and reconstruction which explained more systematically the essence of the program that he had already launched wherever he had the opportunity. He now simply made it clear that every southern state was free to take advantage of his terms. His proclamation required a minimum of ten per cent of the qualified voters of 1860 to take an oath of allegiance. This minority—the "tangible nucleus" that Lincoln had asked for earlier—could then organize a state government, and the President would give it his recognition. Lincoln agreed that it was not an ideal arrangement to have a government supported by only ten per cent of the voters, but it was a beginning, a rallying point to attract others. Concede, he said, that such a government "is only to what it should be as the egg is to the fowl, [but] we shall sooner have the fowl by hatching the egg than by smashing it."

In July 1864 Congress asserted its own jurisdiction over reconstruction when it adopted a bill, introduced by Senator Benjamin F. Wade of Ohio and Representative Henry Winter Davis of Maryland, that outlined a more severe program for the southern states. The Wade-Davis bill provided that each Confederate state was to be ruled temporarily by a military governor, one of whose duties was to supervise the enrollment of the white male citizens. After a majority of those enrolled had taken an oath of allegiance, delegates were to be elected to a state convention which must repudiate secession and abolish slavery. To qualify as a voter or delegate to the convention, however, a Southerner would have to take a second oath—an "ironclad oath"—that he had never voluntarily given support to the Confederacy.

Since Congress passed the Wade-Davis bill on the last

day of the session, Lincoln was able to dispose of it with a pocket veto—that is, to kill it simply by refusing to sign it. In a public proclamation, rather than denounce the terms of the bill he merely explained that he was unwilling "to be inflexibly committed to any single plan of restoration." Indeed, he described the measure as "one very proper plan for the loyal people of any State" and gave them the option of choosing it in preference to his own. Wade and Davis responded with an angry manifesto asserting that "the authority of Congress is paramount" and that the President ought to "confine himself to his executive duties . . . and leave political reorganization to Congress."

But Lincoln ignored this rebuke and adhered to his own plan until his death. In Virginia, throughout the war, he accepted a rump legislature that met in Alexandria behind the Union lines, and a Unionist governor, Francis H. Pierpont, who had been elected by a small minority of loyal voters, as the legal government of the state. In Louisiana and Arkansas, by the spring of 1864, enough citizens had taken the oath of allegiance to form loyal state governments. In Tennessee, by January 1865, a pro-Union government had been established, and the following month the Whig Unionist William G. Brownlow was elected governor. But Lincoln could not persuade Congress to seat Senators and Representatives from the states that had complied with his terms. Thus, at the time of Appomattox, the President and Congress seemed to have reached a stalemate.

Whether Lincoln would have abandoned or altered his program of political reconstruction in the face of severe congressional criticism, there is no way of telling for certain. In his last public speech, on April 11, 1865, he still defended the action he had taken. To repudiate the loyal governments that had been formed, he insisted, would dishearten the thousands of citizens who had taken the oath and returned to their allegiance, and it would delay the re-establishment of normal relations between the southern states and the rest of the Union. And yet Lincoln also hinted several times that he might revise his plan. In his annual message to Congress, December 6, 1864, he warned Southerners that "the time may come—probably will come —when . . . more rigorous measures than heretofore shall be adopted." In his public speech of April 11, he hinted, somewhat vaguely, that his terms were not "inflexible" and that "it may be my duty to make some new announcement to the people of the South." A few days later, at Lincoln's last Cabinet meeting, Secretary of War Edwin M. Stanton presented a plan for the military occupation of the South as the first step toward political reconstruction. Without endorsing it, Lincoln urged Stanton to revise his plan in time for further discussion when the Cabinet next met. The President thus seemed to be wavering slightly. He may well have been near to deciding that the time had come to seek some kind of accommodation with Congress to avoid a disastrous rupture in the Republican party.

The formation of loyal state governments in the South was only the first of several problems that reconstruction embraced. Another was what to do with those who had voluntarily supported the Confederate government and who were therefore subject to arrest, indictment, and trial for treason. Neither Lincoln nor Congress had much taste for a season of mass executions after the war ended, and as early as 1862 Congress decided that such was not to happen. In a sweeping measure that summer, the so-called Second Confiscation Act, Congress provided that treason might be punished by fine and imprisonment as well as by death; moreover, it defined another crime—that of engaging in rebellion or insurrection—whose penalty was fine, imprisonment, and confiscation of property, including slaves. Though this act represented essentially a decision against wholesale executions, its vigorous enforcement nevertheless would have accomplished a vast social revolution in the South; it would have meant the seizure and emancipation of nearly all the slaves and a general redistribution of landed property. In short, it would have resulted in the economic liquidation of the old planter aristocracy.

It would have, except for Lincoln, who had as little taste for social revolutions as for mass executions. He therefore first threatened to veto this measure until Congress provided that the seizure of landed property was to last only during the life of the guilty party, after which the estate would be returned to his heirs. Having gained this point, Lincoln then proceeded to sabotage the measure by failing to enforce it. There were no arrests and indictments for insurrection; there was no emancipation of slaves under its terms; and confiscation proceedings against landed property were negligible. Moreover, Lincoln's proclamation of amnesty and reconstruction of December 8, 1863, had promised those who took the oath of allegiance full pardons that would protect them from the penalties of the Confiscation Act. Certain limited groups, to be sure, were not eligible to take the oath and enjoy the benefits of the general amnesty. These groups included civil officers of the Confederate government, military officers above the rank of colonel, naval officers above the rank of lieutenant, those who had resigned federal judicial offices or seats in Congress, and those who had resigned commissions in the United States Army or Navy. Men in these categories, however, could apply for individual pardons, and Lincoln gave evidence before his death that he would grant them liberally.

Lincoln's terms for the great mass of Confederates, then,

were quite simple: they needed only to take an oath of allegiance to receive full pardons. Most of those in the excepted classes could obtain special pardons with relatively little difficulty. As for the small group of leading rebels—Jefferson Davis, the members of his Cabinet, and a few others—Lincoln was a little perplexed. On one occasion he expressed the hope privately that they would all successfully escape the country and be heard of no more. Death came before he was forced to act, but it is fair to assume that he would have been as generous even with Jefferson Davis as was his successor. Lincoln wanted no martyrs at whose shrines Southerners would worship for generations to come; and he knew, too, that if a vigorous Republican party were to grow in the South it would need the support of many ex-Confederates. That was good politics as well as sweet charity.

A third aspect of reconstruction that required Lincoln's attention was the future of slavery and of the Negro. During the first year of the war he refused to interfere with slavery, and he gave no sign that he would make its abolition a condition of reconstruction.[4] On two occasions he countermanded the orders of military officers who proposed to free the slaves of Confederate sympathizers in their districts; he failed to enforce the emancipation clause of the Confiscation Act; and he refused to accept Negro volunteers in the Union Army for months after Congress authorized him to do so. In the summer of 1862, in a famous reply to an antislavery appeal from Horace Greeley, editor of the New York *Tribune*, Lincoln stated his position with uncommon bluntness: "My paramount object in this struggle is to save the Union and is not either to save

---

[4] In the spring of 1862 Lincoln tried, unsuccessfully, to persuade the Congressmen from the loyal border slave states to work for programs of voluntary gradual emancipation with compensation from the federal treasury.

or to destroy slavery. . . . What I do about slavery, and the colored race, I do because I believe it helps to save the Union; and what I forbear, I forbear because I do not believe it would help to save the Union." Opinions such as these provoked the abolitionist Wendell Phillips to attack Lincoln for waging an aimless war and to denounce him as "a first-rate second-rate man."

But on September 22, 1862, hoping to weaken the rebellion, to satisfy antislavery Northerners, and to strengthen the Union cause abroad, Lincoln issued his preliminary Emancipation Proclamation. He put emancipation into effect in a final proclamation on January 1, 1863, but applied it only to those areas in the South still in rebellion, not to those under federal control. The principle behind it, suggested the London *Spectator*, "is not that a human being cannot justly own another, but that he cannot own him unless he is loyal to the United States." Lincoln's proclamation was not one of his great state papers, for its appeal was not to the rights of man or to any other eternal principles but only to military necessity. Indeed, it may be said that if it was Lincoln's destiny to go down in history as the Great Emancipator, rarely has a man embraced his destiny with greater reluctance than he.

Apparently Lincoln still had not embraced it firmly at the time that he published his Emancipation Proclamation. For in his annual message to Congress in December 1862, he returned to a program that he had always found more to his taste. He proposed that each slave state be given an opportunity to develop its own plan of gradual, compensated emancipation which need not be completed before January 1, 1900. Co-operating states would receive federal financial assistance in the form of interest-bearing government bonds. This slow process, he said, "spares both races from the evils of sudden derangement; while most of those whose habitual course of thought will be disturbed by the measure will have passed away before its consummation. They will never see it." And suppose some state subsequently decided to restore slavery? The only penalty Lincoln suggested was that such state be required to refund the bonds it had received. Thus, even after the Emancipation Proclamation, the total abolition of slavery had not become an indispensable part of Lincoln's plan of reconstruction.

Had it become so a year later, at the time of his proclamation of amnesty and reconstruction? Here he seemed to insist that the abolition of slavery be made a condition of political reconstruction; for his pardons did not restore slave property, and his prescribed oath required support of the acts of Congress and proclamations of the President with reference to slaves. In the states of Louisiana, Arkansas, and Tennessee he put considerable pressure on those forming loyal governments to adopt free-state constitutions. And in July 1864 he offered to entertain any Confederate peace proposal "embracing the restoration of the Union and abandonment of slavery." Yet, a month later, he hinted to a northern conservative critic that he might be willing to settle for less. "To me it seems plain," he wrote, "that saying re-union and the abandonment of slavery would be considered, if offered, is not saying that nothing *else* or *less* would be considered, if offered. . . . If Jefferson Davis wishes . . . to know what I would do if he were to offer peace and re-union, saying nothing about slavery, let him try me."

By 1865, however, some 150,000 Negroes had escaped from slavery and had either joined the Union Army or performed military service by digging trenches and hauling supplies. These Negroes Lincoln now determined must never be returned to bondage. On the ultimate

45

status of the remaining slaves in the Confederate states—more than three million of them—he still may have equivocated a little. In February 1865 Lincoln had a conference with a delegation of Confederates, headed by his old Whig friend, Alexander H. Stephens. Before the meeting Lincoln again made emancipation a condition of peace; but at the meeting, according to Stephens's account, Lincoln was asked what significance the Emancipation Proclamation would have if the southern states agreed to return to the Union. "His own opinion was," related Stephens, "that as the Proclamation was a war measure, and would have effect only from its being an exercise of the war power, as soon as the war ceased, it would be inoperative for the future. It would be held to apply only to such slaves as had come under its operation while it was in active exercise."

Complete and unqualified emancipation came not through action of the President but, necessarily, through a constitutional amendment adopted by Congress. When, in 1865, the Thirteenth Amendment was sent to the states for ratification, Lincoln gave it his support; but had his plan of reconstruction remained in operation, at least a few of the southern states would have had to ratify the amendment to assure its final adoption. If it were ratified, Lincoln still thought it possible to make the transition from slavery to freedom gradual. On several occasions he made it known that he would not object if the southern states resorted to what he called "temporary arrangements for the freed people." He suggested the possibility of some system of apprenticeship to keep the Negroes under white control for a time; a system, as he explained, "by which the two races could gradually live themselves out of their old relation to each other, and both come out better prepared for the new." The system he contemplated would presumably have been under state rather than federal supervision.

Economic or educational assistance for the Negroes, with either state or federal funds, was never a part of Lincoln's program. As for the franchise, Lincoln once hinted to Governor Michael Hahn of Louisiana that it might be wise to permit a few Negroes to vote, "as for instance, the very intelligent, and especially those who have fought gallantly in our ranks." But he hastened to add that this was "only a suggestion." The individual states had to decide who was to be given the franchise; and when Louisiana, Arkansas, and Tennessee gave it to white men only, Lincoln did not regard this as sufficient reason for refusing to recognize their recently formed loyal governments.[5] As long as the Negroes remained in America, he doubted that white men would give them citizenship and equal rights, and he did not ask white men to do so.

But Lincoln never abandoned his hope that the great mass of Negroes could be persuaded to leave the country. He instructed his Secretary of State to determine whether any of the governments in Latin America would agree to accept them, or whether the British or Dutch would have use for them in their American possessions. The only positive result of this diplomatic correspondence was an agreement by the Republic of Haiti to permit two American promoters to settle a group of Negroes on a tiny island, called Ile à Vache, adjacent to its coast. With Lincoln's enthusiastic support the promoters tempted several hundred Negroes to migrate by promising them a life of abundance in a tropical paradise. Instead, the Negro settlers were reduced to virtual bondage and exploited ruthlessly. Within a year, half of them were dead, and the disgraceful episode came to an end when Lincoln, discovering his error, had the survivors brought back to the United States.

---

[5] Most northern states also denied Negroes the franchise. Soon after the war, the voters in Connecticut, Ohio, Michigan, Minnesota, and Kansas rejected proposals for Negro suffrage.

In spite of this fiasco, the President continued to cherish his dream of a separation of the races. "I suppose one of the principal difficulties in the way of colonization," he once admitted, "is that the free colored man cannot see that his comfort would be advanced by it."

Colonization was hardly a statesmanlike solution to the American race problem, as many of Lincoln's contemporaries well understood. Few Negroes favored it, most of their leaders maintaining that their labor had given them as good a claim as white men to American citizenship. Had Lincoln lived to the end of his second administration, he would have been forced to accept the presence of the Negro in his country as a permanent fact; and, given his flexibility, he would doubtless have discovered a more constructive policy than colonization. That he had failed to do so before his death, however, is clear enough.

Lincoln's plan of reconstruction, then, was designed to restore the southern states to the Union with maximum speed and with a minimum of federal intervention in their internal affairs. The great majority of white Southerners would receive amnesty and full power to re-establish loyal state governments; Confederate leaders, with few exceptions, would receive special pardons when they applied for them; the arch rebels, Lincoln hoped, would flee the country. The prewar Whigs, having doubted all along the wisdom of secession, would now be vindicated and would play a powerful role in southern state politics. Since they would need a national organization with which to affiliate, Lincoln stood ready to welcome his old Whig allies into the Republican fold; and, once again, there would be a national party of political conservatives. The Negroes, if they remained, would be governed by the white men among whom they lived, subject only to certain minimum requirements of fair play. Such a program, in Lincoln's mind, was at once humane, politically practical, and constitutionally sound.

For a few years after Lincoln's death, a combination of northern humanitarians and radical Republicans overturned this conservative plan of reconstruction and came near to imposing upon the South a far-reaching social revolution, particularly in the relations of the two races. During the 1870's, however, conservative white men regained control of the southern state governments, and the struggle to give political and legal equality to Negroes was virtually abandoned. Before the reconstruction era had come to a close, the old southern Whigs had been driven into the camp of the Democrats, and the solid Democratic South had been formed—a disaster that Lincoln had tried so hard to prevent.

This being the case, there would seem to be cause to revise somewhat the traditional images we have of the radical Republicans and of Lincoln. In some respects the radical leaders, rather than Lincoln, proved to be the sentimental idealists and the inept politicians; while Lincoln, rather than the radicals, was not only the hardheaded realist but the most skillful politician of them all.

CHAPTER THREE

Andrew Johnson: The Last Jacksonian

On April 15, 1865, the day after the assassination of Abraham Lincoln, a small group of radical Republicans met in Washington to plan their political strategy for the critical times ahead. Among them were Senator Benjamin F. Wade of Ohio, Senator Zachariah Chandler of Michigan, and Representative George W. Julian of Indiana—all members of the powerful congressional Committee on the Conduct of the War, a committee that had vigorously opposed Lincoln's conservative plan of reconstruction. The radicals were determined not to lose the fruits of the war through a "soft" peace—one that would enable the southern rebel leaders to regain the positions of political and economic power they had held before the war. This, the radicals feared, would be the inevitable result of Lincoln's generous terms; and, according to Julian, some of them consequently believed that Lincoln's death was "a godsend to the country." Providence, said Senator Chandler, had kept Lincoln in office as long as he was useful, and then put another and better man in his place.

This new and supposedly better man was Vice President Andrew Johnson, who the radicals believed sympathized with their views. To be sure, Johnson was a Southerner and in prewar politics had been a Democrat—indeed, *still* claimed to be a Democrat. But his recent deeds and utterances about the rebellion make the initial radical confidence in him quite understandable. Like his old hero, Andrew Jackson of Tennessee, Johnson had been a consistent and unqualified Unionist. When Tennessee seceded from the Union, he repudiated the action of his state and remained in his seat in the United States Senate. He even agreed to serve on the Committee on the Conduct of the War, where he worked harmoniously with Wade and Chandler. In 1862, when federal troops occupied much of Tennessee, Lincoln appointed Johnson military governor of the state. Two years later Johnson accepted the vice-presidential nomination on what purported to be a wartime coalition ticket. During the political campaign he delighted the radicals when he castigated the bloated aristocrats of the South and called for their destruction. "I say the traitor has ceased to be a citizen," he cried, "and in joining the rebellion has become a public enemy." In demanding that the rebels be brought to justice, he said many times: "Treason must be made odious and traitors must be punished and impoverished."

When Johnson succeeded to the presidency, the North was in a bitter mood, and his verbal assaults on the southern rebels continued as violently as ever. He offered rewards for the arrest of Jefferson Davis and other Confederate leaders, as well as for the accomplices of John Wilkes Booth. He seemed determined to bring at least some of the prominent Confederates to trial for treason; he showed an interest in the Confiscation Act of 1862 as a device to break up the large southern estates; and he made it clear that he was now committed to the complete abolition of slavery. To a delegation of Pennsylvanians he said: "To those who have deceived, to the conscious, influential traitor, who attempted to destroy the life of the nation—I

51

would say, on you be inflicted the severest penalties of your crimes." In short, Johnson gave no sign of misplaced charity as he prepared to make treason odious and to punish traitors. Ten days after Lincoln's death, Senator Chandler reported that Johnson "is as radical as I am and as fully up to the mark. If he has good men around him, there will be no danger in the future."

In the early days of his administration, Johnson had plenty of good radical friends around him, and he was quite willing to consult with them. His former colleagues on the Committee on the Conduct of the War seemed to expect that they would become his unofficial advisers. They had a most satisfactory interview with him, during which Johnson listened with apparent sympathy while they did most of the talking. At the close of the interview, Senator Wade said happily: "Johnson, we have faith in you. By the gods, there will be no trouble now in running the government." And the beaming President replied with a variation on an old theme: "Treason must be made infamous and traitors must be impoverished."

The radicals departed assuming that the governments Lincoln had organized in four southern states would be repudiated, that the Cabinet would be reorganized, that a few dozen leading rebels would be brought to trial, and that either Congress would be called into special session or political reconstruction would be delayed until Congress met in regular session the following December. In May 1865 one of the radicals, Carl Schurz, made a most favorable assessment of Johnson: "The objects he aims at are all the most progressive friends of human liberty can desire." The New York *Independent*, a radical weekly, rejoiced that Providence had "trained a Southern loyalist in the midst of traitors, a Southern democrat in the midst of aristocrats . . . to be lifted at last to the presidency of the

United States, that he might be charged with the duty of dealing punishment to these self-same assassins of the Union."

Three years later, the radicals in the House of Representatives impeached Johnson for "high misdemeanors," brought him to trial before the Senate, and came within one vote of convicting him and removing him from office. This dramatic shift in Johnson's fortunes resulted in part from subsequent modifications of his ideas about reconstruction, in part from his own limitations as a politician, and in part from the utter failure of the radicals to understand him. Even in the early weeks of apparent harmony, the area of agreement between Johnson and the radicals was quite narrow. The vast expanses of ideological conflict remained concealed, sometimes because the President was less than candid in his interviews with the radicals, sometimes because he and his visitors spoke only in the vaguest generalities. Their common grounds were, first, their mutual desire to suppress the southern rebellion and preserve the Union; second, their mutual support of the Thirteenth Amendment; and, third, their mutual hatred of the southern planter aristocracy and desire to destroy it —and on the last of these, as we shall see, Johnson soon began to waver. Beyond these matters Johnson and the radicals had nothing in common.

The radicals wanted to make the process of political reconstruction relatively slow and complicated. They would keep Southerners out of Congress a while longer in order to reduce their political influence. Meanwhile the radicals would consolidate the position and power of the Republican party, which still had to prove its capacity to survive the sectional crisis that had created it. For a variety of reasons, practical and idealistic, the radicals were determined to use federal power to extend civil and political rights to southern Negroes. In addition, many of them (not all) hoped to preserve the legislation passed during the Civil War for the purpose of encouraging or subsidizing American business enterprise, for example, the national banking act and the protective tariff. None of these goals interested Johnson; indeed, some of them represented evils to be avoided at all costs.

Andrew Johnson, we must remember, was not a Republican, radical or conservative; in spite of his admiration for Lincoln, he was almost as far removed ideologically from the wartime President as he was from the radicals. He did not welcome the vast acceleration of social and economic change for which the Civil War was responsible. In an age of railroads, manufacturing corporations, and commercialized agriculture, Johnson still romanticized the self-sufficient yeoman farmer, still regarded cities as centers of moral decay. In an age of national consolidation, Johnson, in spite of his devotion to the Union, still believed in political decentralization and state rights. In his static world, Thomas Jefferson and Andrew Jackson were sufficient guides to the principles of public morality and the mysteries of political economy; and the Democratic party, in spite of its misguided southern leaders, was the safest custodian of the nation's destiny.

In short, Andrew Johnson practiced the politics of nostalgia; and he discovered in his own career, in which he took infinite pride, full vindication of his old-fashioned social philosophy. Johnson was a self-made man, the embodiment of the American success story, though hardly one of its more attractive products. Born in North Carolina, he endured in his childhood the rigors of extreme poverty. At a tender age, without formal schooling, he was thrust into the world to make his own living. In 1826 he moved across the mountains into East Tennessee, a region of small farms and few slaves, where he settled in the village of Greeneville and opened a tailor shop. There he gained his first taste of success and public recognition: his tailor shop gave him a comfortable income; his wife taught him to write; he read some books; and he joined a debating society. Soon he was in politics, from the first a Jacksonian Democrat, a champion of the village artisans and yeoman farmers, and a bitter foe of the proud and affluent Whigs. "Some day I will show the stuck-up aristocrats who is running the country," he vowed early in his career. "A cheap purse-proud set they are, not half as good as the man who earns his bread by the sweat of his brow."[1]

Johnson's political career was a record of almost unbroken success as he advanced from alderman to mayor of Greenville, to the state legislature, to the federal Congress for five successive terms, to the governorship of Tennessee for two terms, and then in 1857 to the United States Senate. In southern politics he was regarded as something of a radical; and though his understanding of social problems was often primitive, his rhetoric sometimes that of the demagogue, there is no reason to doubt his sincere devotion to the welfare of the common white man of the South. "The people need friends," he said. "They have a great deal to bear." In Tennessee politics his most notable crusade was for a system of free, tax-supported public schools. In national politics he was one of the earliest advocates of a so-called Homestead Act, a measure designed to give actual settlers a gift of 160 acres of land from the public domain. As he pressed for its passage, he repeatedly paraphrased Jefferson's defense of the agrarian

---

[1] "For Johnson, personal fulfillment had long since come to be defined as the fruit of struggle—real, full-bodied, and terrible—against forces specifically organized for thwarting him. . . . Johnson, all his life, had operated as an outsider." Eric L. McKitrick: *Andrew Johnson and Reconstruction* (Chicago, 1960), p. 86.

interest and the Jacksonian's alarm at the passage of the American Arcadian Utopia. "I do not look upon the growth of cities and the accumulation of population around the cities as being the most desirable objects in this country," he said. "Let us try to prevent their further accumulation. . . . I want no miserable city rabble on the one hand; I want no pampered, bloated, corrupt aristocracy on the other; I want the middle portion of society to be built up and sustained. . . . Let us go on interesting men in becoming connected with the soil; . . . prevent their accumulation in the streets of your cities; and in doing this you will dispense with the necessity for your pauper system."

But Johnson's prewar radicalism did not make him an opponent of slavery; in fact, he defended the South's peculiar institution and eventually acquired a few slaves of his own. Ever the democrat, his objection to the slave system was that only a privileged few enjoyed its benefits, and not the mass of white men. In one of the most twisted prayers ever uttered for the welfare of the common man, he once said: "I wish to God every head of a family in the United States had one slave to take the drudgery and menial service off his family." Never did Johnson expand his democratic creed to include the American Negro; like the southern Populists in the late nineteenth century, his was a democracy for white men only. George W. Julian recalled that early in the war Johnson had maintained that emancipation was impossible without immediate colonization. Julian believed that at heart he was "as decided a hater of the negro . . . as the rebels from whom he had separated." But by 1864 Johnson saw that slavery was going to be a casualty of the war, and he accepted this result for two reasons, as he explained: "first, because it is a right in itself, and second, because in the emancipation of the slaves, we break down an odious and dangerous aristocracy."

When Johnson became President and was confronted with the problem of reconstruction, his principal goal at first seemed to be to undermine the southern planter class. But this does not mean that he had at last come to terms with the new centers of political and economic power: the burgeoning cities with their ambitious merchants, manufacturers, and financiers. Still the agrarian, still the backward-looking Jacksonian Democrat, he could see no gain for the common man if a northern moneyed aristocracy replaced a southern landed aristocracy in the seats of power. Johnson was particularly concerned about the influence of a new class of public-security holders that had emerged during the Civil War. After the war he echoed Jefferson's fear of an aristocracy of liquid wealth: "The aristocracy based on $3,000,000,000 of property in slaves . . . has disappeared; but an aristocracy, based on over $2,500,000,000 of national securities, has arisen in the Northern states, to assume that political control which the consolidation of great financial and political interest formerly gave to the slave oligarchy of the late rebel states. . . . We have all read history, and is it not certain, that of all aristocracies mere wealth is the most odious, rapacious, and tyrannical? It goes for the last dollar the poor and helpless have got; and with such a vast machine as this government under its control, that dollar will be fetched. It is an aristocracy that can see in the people only a prey for extortion."

Eventually, Johnson suggested a way to reduce the power of this aristocracy, too. In his last annual message he told Congress that during the war investors had used depreciated paper money to purchase government securities paying high interest rates; thus the government had received in gold only a fraction of the face value of the securities it had issued. Therefore, said Johnson, "it may be assumed that the holders of our securities have already received upon their bonds a larger amount than their original investment." This being the case, he proposed as an equitable settlement the continued payment of the interest on the government debt for sixteen more years, after which the government's obligation should be considered paid in full. "Our national credit should be sacredly observed," Johnson concluded, "but in making provision for our creditors we should not forget what is due to the masses of the people."

Meanwhile, Johnson also made it clear that he regarded the protective tariff as an unjust burden upon consumers; the national banking system as a dangerous monopoly; and the sale of timber and mineral lands from the public domain to private corporations as a betrayal of the homestead policy adopted in 1862. "The public domain," he said, "is a national trust, set apart and held for the general welfare upon principles of equal justice, and not to be bestowed as a special privilege upon a favored class." In pure Jacksonian rhetoric, he denounced those who sought to obtain special favors from government. "Monopolies, perpetuities, and class legislation," he insisted, "are contrary to the genius of free government. . . . Wherever monopoly attains a foothold, it is sure to be a source of danger, discord, and trouble. . . . The government is subordinate to the people; but, as the agent and representative of the people, it must be held superior to monopolies, which in themselves ought never to be granted."

Johnson aimed his blows at the southern lords of the manor, then, not to give aid and comfort to the new masters of capital, but to strengthen the position of the

American yeomanry. To him, as to Jefferson, they were "the chosen people of God." Time after time they had been betrayed by powerful combinations of vested interests who sought to control the government for their own selfish ends: first by Hamilton and the Federalist commercial aristocracy, until Jefferson restored the government to the tillers of the soil; then by Nicholas Biddle and the national banking interest, until Jackson destroyed them with a crushing veto; then by John C. Calhoun and the planter aristocracy, whom Johnson had been fighting during his long political career.

But Johnson was now in a position to make this time of political reconstruction a time of triumph for the yeoman class. This was the class that he hoped to bring to power in the New South—the class whose interests he would make decisive in the formulation of public policy. For this end, a reorganized and strengthened Democratic party, cleansed of its disloyal prewar leadership, would be a reliable instrument; and with an agrarian-oriented Democracy in control, the country would return to first principles and paradise would be regained.[2]

Unfortunately for Johnson, the radical Republicans, especially those from the states of the Northeast, had a somewhat different vision of paradise. As the radicals gradually realized what Johnson's goals actually were, they reluctantly decided that their opposition to executive leadership would have to be renewed.

The irreconcilable differences between their respective

---

[2] For a while, in 1866, Johnson considered forming a new national conservative party. Secretary of State William H. Seward had been urging a "reorganization of parties that would attract the support of Southerners and of Northern Democrats by a speedy and generous restoration of the secession states." LaWanda and John H. Cox: *Politics, Principle, and Prejudice, 1865–1866* (New York, 1963), p. 222. But this was after Johnson's program had clearly failed; and, in any case, nothing came of the idea.

programs made conflict inevitable, but this alone does not explain the level of extreme violence it ultimately reached. Johnson's background and personality—his shortcomings as a politician—were also responsible for the numerous unseemly incidents of his administration. This is not to suggest that the radicals were guiltless, for the language they used in their attacks upon the President was often inexcusable. But Johnson, if he hoped to exercise executive leadership, could ill afford the luxury of answering in kind. Unfortunately, this was a luxury he could not resist, even at the cost of compromising the dignity of his office. Unlike Lincoln, he was not a master of men—not even master of himself.

Johnson's origins, as we have seen, were as humble as Lincoln's, his rise to fame just as spectacular. But Lincoln made his log-cabin, rail-splitting background, his embodiment of the American success story, a political asset; Johnson made it a liability, for he was heavy-handed in exploiting it. His humble origin and the scorn and contempt the planter class had heaped upon him in earlier years made him bitter, pugnacious, and self-assertive. He had no ease, no grace, no self-confidence. Many times he permitted radicals, with whose views he disagreed, to depart from an interview convinced that there was no disagreement at all. "He listened so attentively," Carl Schurz once reported, "that I was almost sure he would heed my advice." Moreover, his lack of self-confidence made him indecisive at crucial times. Gideon Welles, Johnson's Secretary of the Navy, noted that "it has been the misfortune, the weakness, the great error of the President to delay,—hesitate before acting." Yet Welles knew of no man who was more firm once he had taken a stand. Johnson's firmness, however, took the form of inflexibility, for there was in him a streak of stiff stubbornness that served him ill. Having made up his mind, he would not compromise; he would not yield a minor point to gain a major objective; he was utterly devoid of tact.

Early in his career Johnson had won a reputation as an orator, but his was a brand of oratory fashioned in the rough school of East Tennessee politics, where the graceful rhetoric, rounded periods, and classical allusions of a Jefferson Davis had little appeal. Johnson had waged his political campaigns in basic English; and after he became President he reverted to these tactics easily, almost instinctively, in the heat of debate. His enemies did not find it difficult to provoke him to verbal indiscretions.

Radical disillusionment with Johnson began as soon as he ceased gnashing his teeth and shaking his fist at rebels and started actually to formulate reconstruction policies. The war was over now; the South was defeated; and the political realities called for something more than bold posturing and terrible threats. Southerners, stunned in defeat, waited to hear the terms with which they would have to comply. How smoothly reconstruction would proceed depended in part on how decisively federal authorities acted immediately after the surrender. Early in May, Schurz wrote Sumner: "If we only make a vigorous start in the right direction the problem will be easily solved. But if too much latitude is given to the mischievous elements in the South for the next few weeks, it will be exceedingly difficult to set matters right again."

Johnson responded with a series of public statements and executive proclamations that left the radicals momentarily stunned, because they seemed so utterly contrary to his former position. The new President, it now appeared, was as convinced as Lincoln had been that reconstruction was the responsibility of the Executive Department and not of Congress. He did not propose to call Congress into special session, or to delay reconstruction until December when Congress would meet in regular session. Rather, he would start and finish it in the seven months before Congress assembled and then present Congress with a *fait accompli*. Nor did he propose to reorganize Lincoln's conservative Cabinet, or to accept the radicals as his unofficial advisers. Instead, he proposed, like Lincoln, to go it alone; and if Lincoln's position was vulnerable for ignoring Congress, Johnson's position was well-nigh indefensible. The circumstances that brought him to the head of the Executive Department gave him no popular mandate and enabled indignant and disrespectful radicals to refer to him as "His Accidency the President."

Nevertheless, Johnson announced that he would continue to apply Lincoln's plan of reconstruction, though, in fact, he modified its terms and significantly changed its purpose. On May 9, 1865, he officially recognized the Pierpont government as the legal government of Virginia. Three weeks later, on May 29, he formalized his program in two proclamations. In the first of these he prescribed an oath of allegiance that the mass of southern people would be permitted to take; those who took it would receive amnesty and pardon and the restoration of all rights of property, except slaves, unless confiscation proceedings had already been instituted. In other words, taking the oath brought with it the recovery of civil and political rights, immunity from prosecution for treason or conspiracy, and exemption from the provisions of the Confiscation Act.

Johnson, however, listed fourteen classes of persons who were not entitled to the benefits of his amnesty, and these exceptions were more numerous than Lincoln's. While the war was still in progress, he had said: "Many humble men, the peasantry and yeomanry of the South, who have been decoyed, or perhaps driven into rebellion, may look forward with reasonable hope for an amnesty. But the intelligent and influential leaders must suffer." The exceptions, as one would expect, included Confederate civil and military officers; but the thirteenth classification was by far the most interesting and significant. For here Johnson acted as the class-conscious plebeian—the radical agrarian who was setting out to remake the social and political life of the South. All those who had supported the Confederacy and whose taxable property was valued at $20,000 or more were barred from taking the Johnson oath and obtaining amnesty. "You know perfectly well," Johnson told a delegation of Virginians, "it was the wealthy men of the South who dragooned the people into secession." These men were to have no part in political reconstruction. If power were to be transferred to the yeomanry, this would be a practical step in that direction; for without pardons the large property holders would be politically disenfranchised and still liable to confiscation proceedings. But all was not lost for them, for Johnson did provide that members of the excepted classes could apply for special pardons; he promised that each of them would receive a fair hearing.

The second proclamation of May 29 outlined the steps for the formation of loyal state governments.[3] In each of the southern states the President would appoint a provisional governor whose duty it would be to call a state convention and supervise the election of delegates to it. Only those who could qualify under the state laws in effect in 1860 and who had taken the amnesty oath would be entitled to vote or stand for election. The convention could then prescribe permanent voting and office-holding

---

[3] The proclamation of May 29 applied only to North Carolina. Within the next few weeks similar proclamations put the same program into effect in the other southern states where reconstruction had not yet begun. As in Virginia, Johnson accepted the Lincoln governments in Arkansas, Louisiana, and Tennessee.

requirements, after which an election would be held for a regular governor, state legislature, and members of Congress. Less formally, Johnson demanded that the southern states proclaim the illegality of their ordinances of secession, repudiate all Confederate debts, and ratify the Thirteenth Amendment. The process of political reconstruction would then be completed, and the President would revoke martial law and withdraw the federal troops.

This is the program that Johnson launched in the southern states during the summer of 1865, while the congressional radicals looked on helplessly. Within a few months the conventions had finished their business, the state elections had been held, and presidential proclamations had retired the provisional governors and turned political power over to the newly elected governors and legislatures. In December, when Congress assembled, Johnson announced that the process of reconstruction was completed. The southern people, he said, had returned to their allegiance in good faith; the southern states had been restored to their proper position in the Union; federal courts, customs houses, and post offices were open; and it was the duty of Congress now to seat southern Senators and Representatives.[4] In the South, he concluded, "the aspect of affairs is more promising than, in view of all the circumstances, could well have been expected." In short, Johnson congratulated himself on a job well done.

Or at least that was his public posture. Whether inwardly he was as pleased with the outcome of his reconstruction program as outwardly he pretended to be may well be doubted. Eventually Congress rejected the John-

---

[4] In Texas Johnson's program of reconstruction was not completed until the following spring. On August 20, 1866, Johnson formally proclaimed "that the insurrection . . . is at an end, and is henceforth to be so regarded."

son governments in the South, formulated its own policies, and at last, in 1867, put in motion a new plan of recon-struction—thereby wounding the President as painfully as he had previously wounded Congress. The historical tradition, therefore, is that the radical repudiation of presidential reconstruction represented Andrew Johnson's ultimate defeat and humiliation. But this is dubious his-tory, because the President had already suffered a devastating defeat even before Congress assembled. Actu-ally, the radical attack upon him saved him from having to face up to his own personal failure. For Johnson, in implementing his reconstruction program, had somehow either lost sight of his original goals or lacked the firm-ness and political skill he would have needed to attain them.

At the outset he had taken a bold stand. The prewar leaders of the South, he had said, "must be conquered and a new set of men brought forward who are to vitalize and develop the Union feeling in the South." Moreover, the great plantations "must be seized and divided into small portions and sold to honest, industrious men." But by December 1865 Johnson's dream of an agrarian Utopia had been lost; he was almost the prisoner of the men he had set out to destroy; and he was com-mitted to a swift termination of political reconstruction in the name of state rights. His resort to narrow con-stitutionalism to defend what was now an aimless policy was for all practical purposes a declaration of political bankruptcy.[5]

---

[5] Johnson's own plan of reconstruction—he preferred the term *restora-tion*—was not based on a strict state-rights constitutional position. For he required the southern states to do certain things, such as repudi-ating Confederate debts and abolishing slavery, before they could participate in the government. He used the state-rights argument only when Congress laid down additional terms. Thaddeus Stevens, on several occasions, accurately pointed to Johnson's inconsistency.

Why, then, did Johnson fail? He failed primarily because of an erroneous assumption about the attitude of
the southern white masses toward the planter class. From
the beginning of his political career, Johnson had believed that the southern yeomanry were the helpless
victims of a ruling aristocracy, waiting hopefully for new
leaders who would champion their cause. Secession, he
repeatedly claimed, had been engineered by a small clique
of planter politicians against the will of the majority. But
after the war, with the planter aristocracy defeated and
discredited, with Johnson in a position to give the yeomanry their chance, he expected them to find leadership
that would enable them to control the southern conventions and state governments organized under his plan of
reconstruction.

Unfortunately, Johnson had become the captive of his
own Jacksonian rhetoric and vastly oversimplified the
problem he faced. To be sure, there had been tensions in
the relations between farmers and planters in the ante-
bellum South; among the masses there had always been
an undercurrent of envy and resentment. But much of
the time these unsophisticated rural folk had also ex-
hibited toward the planters a certain measure of respect
and admiration, and a willingness to accept their political
leadership. Though some undemocratic political practices
still survived in the South, the great majority of white
non-slaveholders nevertheless had the franchise, and the
aristocracy had to exert its influence within an essentially
democratic political framework. It was the wealth, education, and self-confidence of the slaveholders—their mastery
of the techniques that bring political success in a democracy—that enabled them to exert great influence on their
humble neighbors. They had not dragged a reluctant
people out of the Union in 1861, for the vast majority of
the white yeomen in the Confederate states had favored

secession. And the vast majority still seemed to be satisfied with the old leadership when the war ended and the Confederacy collapsed.

Nothing, then, had really changed in the South when Johnson prepared to establish new state governments; there was no significant grass-roots movement for a change in political leadership. According to John W. De Forest, a Union officer, southern politics still reflected "the somewhat feudal, somewhat patriarchal, social position of the large planter. . . . Every community has its great man . . . around whom his fellow citizens gather when they want information, and to whose monologues they listen with a respect akin to humility. . . . [Everywhere] that I went . . . I found the chivalrous Southron still under the domination of his ancient leaders." And the southern elections of 1865 bore him out. In Mississippi the new legislature did reflect an increase in the power of the small landholders; and in Tennessee the Unionists won complete control. But in general the planters and Confederate leaders captured the Johnson governments. Many of the new governors and legislators had been active rebels and boasted of their wartime activities in their political campaigns. Scores of them belonged to one or another of the categories that Johnson had excluded from his general amnesty. The new governor of South Carolina, James L. Orr, had served in the Confederate Senate; the new governor of Mississippi, Benjamin G. Humphreys, had been a Confederate brigadier general. The great majority of those elected to Congress had been Confederate military officers, Cabinet officers, or Congressmen; among them was Alexander H. Stephens of Georgia, Confederate Vice President, elected to the United States Senate.

Johnson poured out his bitter disappointment to William W. Holden, his provisional governor in North

Carolina. In that state six of the seven men elected to Congress were not entitled to take the amnesty oath, and many members of the legislature had not yet received presidential pardons. "The results of the recent elections in North Carolina," Johnson told Holden, "have greatly damaged the prospects of the State in the restoration of its governmental relations. Should the action and spirit of the legislature be in the same direction it will greatly increase the mischief already done and might be fatal."

Johnson was then forced to make a crucial decision. Somehow he had to deal with Southerners in the excepted classes who had been denied the benefits of his amnesty proclamation but had nevertheless been elected to public office. Since they symbolized the defeat of his southern program, he might have refused to permit them to take office and called for new elections. He might even have concluded that his attempt at political reconstruction was premature and that federal control would have to continue for a while longer. Clearly there had not been time enough for the recruitment of new southern leadership and for the organizational work that was needed if Johnson's goals were to be achieved. But Johnson did none of these things. Instead he issued special pardons in wholesale lots—to delegates to the state conventions, to governors, to members of the legislatures, to Congressmen-elect, and to mayors and other local officials. Planters, prewar politicians, Confederate military leaders often had merely to call on the President—sometimes only to write to him— to get the desired pardons. Altogether Johnson had granted some 13,500 special pardons when, on September 7, 1867, he issued a second amnesty proclamation which left only a few hundred former Confederates unpardoned.[6]

---

[6] In a third proclamation, on July 4, 1868, Johnson granted pardons to all but a handful of ex-rebels, and the following Christmas Day he pardoned these last few as well.

III: *Andrew Johnson: The Last Jacksonian*

"Had it not been for the special pardons," an angry Georgia Unionist complained to Thaddeus Stevens, "the genuine union men could of carried the state and sent original union men to Congress." In Virginia, a Union officer told a congressional committee, pardoned rebels "seem to have assumed . . . political control, and to exercise an influence upon society that they did not before they received those pardons. . . . The Union people were in the minority after these secessionists got their pardons, and had to take back seats."

Moreover, Johnson soon lost interest in land reform through confiscation. By the end of 1865 he had dropped all but a few flagrant cases, and early the next year he abandoned confiscation entirely. His Attorney General ruled that the Confiscation Act of 1862 was valid only in wartime and could not be enforced after the restoration of peace.

In short, Johnson had given up. There would be no social or political revolution in the South after all. Southern Unionists and others who had hoped to bar the prewar politicians from positions of power in the New South now turned against the President; his former enemies, who had despised him in earlier years, now came to his defense. A South Carolina planter, Henry W. Ravenel, described this remarkable change: "How hard it is to know really the character of public men," he wrote. "I had always heard of [President Johnson] as a demagogue and pot house politician in Tennessee of the lowest order. . . . I freely acknowledge that my first impressions of him [were] erroneous. . . . [He] has placed himself in opposition to the radicals . . . and by his acts and influence has shielded the South from [their] vindictive policy."

Why Johnson abandoned his goals so precipitately, why he first disenfranchised the southern aristocracy by denying them amnesty and then gave them individual pardons

69

with such unseemly haste, has always been something of a mystery. Perhaps Johnson, being a confirmed democrat, saw no alternative once they had been duly elected to office. Perhaps his growing fear of northern capitalists eventually caused him to see the value of the planter class as a countervailing political force. Perhaps he simply lacked the iron will, the quality of ruthlessness, he would have needed to achieve his goals. Perhaps he was, after all, at heart a conservative who shrank from the prospect of political turmoil and economic upheaval once he had experienced the sobering responsibility of power. Perhaps he was influenced by his adroit Secretary of State, William H. Seward, who urged a generous reconstruction policy to facilitate the creation of a great national conservative party. Perhaps his ambition for a presidential nomination in 1868 diverted him from his original course.

All these may have been important reasons for Johnson's behavior, but there is still another that needs to be considered. It is that Johnson, in 1865, betrayed a weakness that is common among men of his background and experience, though far from universal. The memory of his early poverty, the scars he bore from his political battles, the snubs he had received from the haughty planter aristocracy, all had left him with a raw ego and a craving for recognition and respect.[7] Like the southern common people for whom he spoke, Johnson's resentment of the planter class was, after all, combined with a certain grudging admiration. If his vanity demanded that he gain recognition and respect, then nothing could satisfy him more than forcing this class to seek mercy from his hands. By denying amnesty to all Confederate leaders and large

---

[7] These characteristics were evident in nearly all of his speeches, before and after he became President.

property-holders and requiring them to apply to him for special pardons, this is precisely what he obliged them to do. Those who had scorned him were now flattering him, appealing to his generosity, begging for the franchise and the protection of their property—but influencing his policy as well.

As early as June 5, 1865, Schurz warned Sumner that southern delegations were "crowding into Washington" and that the President was permitting "his judgment to be controlled by their representations." A few weeks later, Henry D. Cooke wrote Representative John Sherman of Ohio that Washington was "full of Southern people, and the President is occupied half his time in receiving delegations from Dixie. The effect of this is an increasingly evident leaning towards a more conservative policy." On September 11, representatives of nine southern states visited Johnson for the purpose, as one of them explained, "of manifesting the sincere respect and regard they entertain for you . . . and to say . . . that they have great confidence in your wisdom to heal the wounds that have been made, and in your disposition to exercise all the leniency which can be commended by a sound and judicious policy." With an air of self-righteousness Johnson reminded his visitors of the "taunts, the jeers, the scowls, with which I was treated." He had warned the misguided southern leaders, and now he had "lived to see the realization of my predictions and the fatal error of those whom I vainly essayed to save from the results I could not but foresee."

For Johnson this was obviously an intoxicating experience, and he became a little giddy as delegation after delegation of contrite Southerners assured him that the fate of the South was in his hands. Before long he began to sound less and less like an angry plebeian, more and more

71

like a mellow patrician in his defense of southern rights. No longer did he speak of punishing traitors and making treason odious; rather, he said: "I did not expect to keep out all who were excluded from the amnesty, or even a large number of them, but I intended they should sue for pardon, and so realize the enormity of their crime." The pardons flowed from the President's office to men who realized nothing of the sort; to men who accepted him now, humbled themselves before him, showered him with praise—and captured his governments in the South. Why, then, did Johnson fail? The answer, in part, is that the planter politicians proved to be more skillful than he; finding his weakness, they exploited his vanity and thus defeated him with remarkable ease.

More than that: after reducing the Johnson plan of reconstruction to a shambles, the planter politicians maneuvered the President into so compromising a position that he was obliged to side with them against the radical Republicans. To have done otherwise would have been to admit failure and, in consequence, to invite Congress to take command. This was a humiliation that Johnson could not bear, and to avoid it he boldly assured Congress that his program had been a complete success. He defended the men who controlled the governments he had created. He claimed that they were now thoroughly loyal and repentant; that they had accepted the results of the war and were acting in good faith; that their feelings toward Northerners were nothing but friendly; and that they were dealing fairly with their former slaves. Had all this been true, Johnson's position still would have been strong, and he would doubtless have been able to force Congress eventually to recognize his governments in the South. But all this was far from true, for the southern politicians whom Johnson defended were discrediting him by their irresponsible behavior. As a result, they were to blame not only for defeating his reconstruction plans but also for strengthening the radicals and making certain their ultimate victory over the President.

In December 1865, after listening to Johnson's message to Congress, the radicals claimed that he had grossly misrepresented conditions in the South. The radicals insisted that the men who had won control of his southern state governments were still rebels at heart; that they had not been reconciled to defeat and would seize the first opportunity to launch another rebellion; that they were persecuting northern settlers; and that they were reducing the Negroes to slavery once more.

Johnson and the radicals both searched for evidence to prove their cases, and both found numerous eyewitnesses to support them. General Grant, Harvey M. Watterson, and Benjamin C. Truman, a pro-Johnson newspaper correspondent, toured the South and submitted reports highly pleasing to Johnson. Grant concluded "that the mass of thinking men of the South accept the present situation of affairs in good faith." Writing in April 1866, Truman reported that "the great, substantial, and prevailing element" in the South "is more loyal now than it was at the end of the war." Johnson also sent Carl Schurz on a tour of the South, but Schurz's preliminary reports, in the form of letters to the President and to the Boston *Advertiser,* indicated that his observations would be far more pleasing to the radicals. Johnson did not ask Schurz for a report, but Schurz wrote one anyway; and the radicals, after forcing Johnson to submit it to Congress, used it to good advantage. Early in 1866, scores of witnesses testified before the Joint Committee on Reconstruction, which Congress had created the previous December, and most of them gave aid and comfort to the radicals. In addition, many southern Unionists wrote private letters to the President and to Republican members of Congress complaining bitterly about conditions in the South under the Johnson governments. None of these reports was free from bias of one kind or another, but in many ways Schurz's report was the best of them. Though partial to the radicals, it was systematically organized, relatively restrained, remarkably perceptive, and reasonably candid.

From the conflicting testimony a few generalizations about conditions in the South and the attitudes of Southerners would seem to be valid. Southerners did understand that they had been defeated, and they were co-operating in the establishment of new state governments under Johnson's formula. Rumors that they were plotting another rebellion were pure nonsense. Most of those who were eligible to take Johnson's oath of allegiance hastened to do so; most of those who were not eligible petitioned for special pardons. As Schurz reported, whatever differences may exist among Southerners, "on one point they are agreed: further resistance to the power of the national government is useless, and submission to its authority a matter of necessity."

However, a large number of Southerners were bitter in defeat; few of them would have agreed that what they had done in 1861 was morally wrong, or that the right had triumphed. Benjamin C. Truman noted that "boisterous demagogues" and "reckless editors" were still pouring forth "obnoxious utterances." Schurz found among the southern people "an utter absence of national feeling." Loyalty consisted of "submission to necessity," and submission was advocated as "the only means by which they could rid themselves of the federal soldiers and obtain once more control of their own affairs." Certainly Southerners were not conceding any more than they had to.

Many of them were exhibiting a strong hostility toward Northerners who had settled in the South during or after the war, and, if anything, an even stronger hostility toward Southerners who had been Unionists.

Moreover, it would be far from the truth to say that white Southerners generally were reconciled to the Negro's new status as a freedman. Many former slaveholders shared the regret of Louis Manigault, a Georgia planter, that the "former mutual and pleasing feeling of Master towards Slave and vice versa is now as a dream of the past." The whites intensely resented the presence of Negro troops in the South; the more brutal whites committed countless acts of violence against the freedmen; and men of all classes considered any deviation on the part of Negroes from the subservience of slavery days as "insolence." Carl Schurz met planters who were trying to deal fairly with the freedmen, but he also presented overwhelming evidence that the Negroes needed federal protection. In North Carolina, reported General G. F. Granger, "the poor negro hears on all sides . . . that he is after all notwithstanding his freedom, now and forever more, 'nothing but a damned nigger.' " R. W. Flournoy of Mississippi, a large slaveholder before the war, now genuinely concerned about the freedman's welfare, told Thaddeus Stevens: "To leave the negro to be dealt with by those whose prejudices are of the most bitter character against him, will be barbarous."

Given the prevailing attitudes—all of them human enough and quite understandable—southern political leaders made many tactless blunders, as even the none-too-tactful President himself privately recognized. In the fall of 1865, Gideon Welles, a firm supporter of Johnson's reconstruction program, recorded in his diary quite a different picture of conditions in the South than the one to which the administration was officially committed: "The tone of sentiment and action of [the] people of the South," he wrote, "is injudicious and indiscreet in many respects. . . . The entire South seem to be stupid and vindictive, know not their friends, and are pursuing just the course which their opponents, the Radicals, desire. I fear a terrible ordeal awaits them in the future."

Most of these blunders, which shocked the northern people and strengthened the radicals, reflected the pride of the southern people and expressed their belief in the justness of their cause. The North, wrote Confederate General Wade Hampton of South Carolina, had no right to expect that the South would "at once profess unbounded love to that Union from which for four years she tried to escape." It was, therefore, perhaps too much to expect Southerners to welcome Northerners and admit them to their homes, or to reward southern Unionists for opposing the Confederacy by electing them to public office. Appointments in the Johnson governments also went to ex-Confederates. A Louisiana Unionist complained to Schurz that the offices "are now being distributed to men who held commissions in the rebel army, who signed the ordinance of secession . . . [and] who took a leading part in the rebel movement; you can see them now as judges, sheriffs, and important officers of the new state." In January 1866, *Harper's Weekly* reported indignantly that General Hampton "was received with all the honors by the Legislature of Alabama, and responded to their acclamations by eulogizing the noble and heroic effort of the people of that State to destroy the United States Government."

Several southern conventions still would not agree that secession had been illegal; therefore, they merely repealed, rather than repudiated, the ordinances of secession and thus yielded nothing in principle. The Johnson legislature in Arkansas voted pensions for Confederate veterans; Mississippi refused to ratify the Thirteenth Amendment; South Carolina refused to repudiate the Confederate debt. Under the aegis of Johnsonian reconstruction was born a popular type of postwar southern politician who played the role of professional ex-Confederate and Yankee-baiter.

Most damaging were the policies pursued by the Johnson governments toward the Negroes. Though Johnson, like Lincoln, first hoped to eliminate the race issue by colonizing the Negroes outside the United States, by 1865 he seemed to have realized that the Negroes were going to be a permanent part of the southern population. Yet his reconstruction terms did not require the southern states to deal fairly with the Negroes; his only demand was that they accept the abolition of slavery. Beyond this, he thought, the federal government had no jurisdiction; questions of education, social relationships, and civil and political rights must be settled by the individual states. On one occasion Johnson suggested to Provisional Governor William L. Sharkey of Mississippi that the vote be given to Negroes who could meet literacy and property requirements. This, he explained, would "disarm" the radicals, who were "wild upon negro franchise." But he did not make this a condition of recognition. "My position as President," he once said, "is different from what it would be if I were in Tennessee. There I should try to introduce negro suffrage gradually. . . . It would not do to let the negroes have universal suffrage now; it would breed a war of races." Actually, Johnson was never enthusiastic about Negro suffrage, because he feared that the votes of these economically helpless people would be controlled by the large landholders. And since Johnson showed virtually no interest in the Negroes—no desire to give them federal protection—he helped to push them into the arms of the radicals.

So did the Johnson governments in the South, for all of them restricted the suffrage to the whites. Governor Humphreys of Mississippi affirmed in his inaugural address "that ours is and it shall ever be, a government of white men." In Louisiana a state Democratic convention resolved that "we hold this to be a Government of White People, made and to be perpetuated for the exclusive political benefit of the White Race, and . . . that the people of African descent cannot be considered as citizens of the United States." In short, one vital prop of Negro freedom —political rights—was withheld.

A second prop—education—was also denied the Negroes. Schurz observed that "the popular prejudice is almost as bitterly set against the negro's having the advantage of education as it was when the negro was a slave. . . . Hundreds of times I heard the old assertion repeated, that 'learning will spoil the nigger for work,' and that 'negro education will be the ruin of the South.' Another most singular notion still holds a potent sway over the minds of the masses —it is, that the elevation of the blacks will be the degradation of the whites." As a result of these attitudes, none of the Johnson governments made any effective provision for Negro education. Moreover, white public opinion was generally hostile to the efforts of private benevolent societies to establish Negro schools.

The Johnsonians also made quite clear what they thought the Negro's economic role in the New South should be. The future envisioned for him was that of an illiterate, unskilled, propertyless, agricultural worker. A delegate to the Texas constitutional convention said: "I concede them nothing but the station of 'hewers of wood and drawers of water.' " This design, of course, was meant to assure the whites of a perpetual supply of cheap labor, but it also reflected their belief that the Negro had the capacity for nothing better. John B. Baldwin of Virginia told the Joint Committee on Reconstruction: "I do not believe that, as a race, they will ever have the persistence of purpose, or the energy, or the intellectual vigor to rise to anything like intellectual equality with the white race. I think that they will get along very well in the ordinary domestic relations, as servants and inferiors." An Alabama patriarch, seeking a remedy for what he called the evils of abolition, urged Southerners to "secure the services of the negroes, teach them their places, and how to keep them, and convince them at last that we are indeed their best friends." The Negro, he said, "is proud to call you master yet. In the name of humanity, let him do so."

The leaders of the Johnson governments combined these attitudes with a general conviction that the Negro would not work without compulsion of some kind. The Negro's innate indolence, said a Virginia planter, could only be dealt with by "prudent legislation." This conviction produced the best-remembered enactments of the Johnson legislatures: the so-called Black Codes framed to control the Negroes and severely restrict their civil rights. The crucial point about these codes was their ultimate purpose. They were not designed to help the Negro through the admittedly difficult transition from the status of slave to that of a responsible freeman. They were not intended to prepare him for a constructive role in the social, political, and economic life of the South. Few believed that such a role was possible. Rather, the purpose of the Black Codes was to keep the Negro, as long as possible, exactly what he was: a propertyless rural laborer under strict controls, without political rights, and with inferior legal rights. As Schurz quite accurately explained them, they were "a striking embodiment of the idea that although the former owner has lost his individual right of property in the former slave, 'the blacks at large belong to the whites at large.' " To put it bluntly, the Black Codes placed the Negro in a kind of twilight zone between slavery and freedom.

Among their numerous provisions, the codes legalized Negro marriages, permitted Negroes to hold and dispose of property, to sue and be sued. They also took steps toward the establishment of racial segregation in public places. They prohibited inter-racial marriages, prohibited Negroes from serving on juries or testifying against white men, and re-enacted many of the criminal provisions of the prewar slave codes. In the economic sphere, South Carolina prohibited Negroes from entering any employment except agricultural labor without a special license; Mississippi would not permit them to buy or rent farm land; these states and others provided that Negroes found without lawful employment were to be arrested as vagrants and auctioned off or hired to landholders who would pay their fines. Louisiana required all Negro agricultural laborers to make contracts with landholders during the first ten days of January; once made, the contracts were binding for the year. Thereafter the Negroes were not permitted to leave their places of employment without permission. A Negro who refused to labor for his employer was to be arrested and put to forced labor on public works without compensation until he agreed to go back to his job.

This return to a modified form of involuntary servitude caused Negroes, at numerous meetings, to call on Congress for protection. The Chicago *Tribune* warned Mississippi that the North would convert her "into a frog pond" before permitting slavery to be re-established. A minority of cautious Southerners had advised against the Black Codes —a Mississippian was "amazed at such stupidity." Eventually military officers suspended much of the Mississippi code and threw out the entire South Carolina code.

But President Johnson had acquiesced in the Black Codes without a murmur. On December 18, 1865, in a special message to the Senate, he made an oblique reference to them as "measures . . . to confer upon freedmen the privileges which are essential to their comfort, protection, and security." Problems, he added, "are naturally to be expected from the great and sudden change in the relations between the two races; but systems are gradually developing themselves under which the freedman will receive the protection to which he is justly entitled, and, by means of his labor, make himself a useful and independent member of the community in which he has a home."

As Congress began to take a hand, Johnson's control over the process of reconstruction came to an end. For him one can scarcely imagine an end more disastrous. A program that began with the dream of a new day for the southern yeomanry terminated with the landlords fashioning a new kind of bondage for their black laborers, and with Johnson their witting or unwitting ally. Such a settlement the radical Republicans refused to accept; and before Congress had finished, it had armed the federal government with power to make Negro emancipation more than nominal. If this could have been accomplished in any other way, the alternative never appeared during the era of reconstruction.

And yet, a persistent historical tradition holds that the radical Republicans were responsible for the tragic form that southern race relations took in the late nineteenth and early twentieth centuries. According to this tradition, everything was working smoothly—the two races were making a harmonious adjustment—under Johnson's wise program, until the radicals intervened. The truth is that, before the radical program began, the Johnson governments themselves had introduced the whole pattern of disenfranchisement, discrimination, and segregation into the postwar South. And there, quite possibly, matters might still stand, had Andrew Johnson had his way.

CHAPTER FOUR

Triumph of the Radicals

The first session of the Thirty-ninth Congress assembled on December 4, 1865, more than seven months after Andrew Johnson became President. At the outset this Congress contained four roughly defined political groups, unequal in size and in the quality of their leadership. First, there was a small, disorganized, demoralized Democratic minority whose leaders, insofar as it had any, were Senator Thomas A. Hendricks of Indiana and Representative Samuel S. Cox of Ohio. Though the Democrats first looked upon President Johnson as an apostate because of his identification with Lincoln in 1864, they soon gave him their support. Second, there was a rather feeble band of conservative Republicans, which included Senators James R. Doolittle of Wisconsin, James Dixon of Connecticut, and Edgar Cowan of Pennsylvania, and Representative Henry J. Raymond of New York, all of whom were already quite solidly committed to Johnson. Third, there was a faction of radical Republicans, more numerous than either of the first two groups but still a decided minority even in the Republican party. Among those who could be identified clearly as radicals were Senators Charles Sumner and Henry Wilson of Massachusetts, Benjamin F. Wade of Ohio, and Zachariah Chandler of Michigan; and Representatives Thaddeus Stevens, William Kelley, and John M. Broomall of Pennsylvania, George S. Boutwell of Massachusetts, James M. Ashley of Ohio, George W. Julian of Indiana, and James F. Wilson of Iowa. Finally, there were the moderate Republicans—the largest group in this Congress—who leaned slightly toward Johnson but were nevertheless still wavering between the radical and conservative camps. Senator John Sherman of Ohio, brother of General Sherman, was a representative moderate.[1]

The moderate Republicans held the balance of power; whichever group they gravitated toward would ultimately win control of Congress. In December Johnson still had the advantage, not only because the moderates were within his grasp, but also because his reconstruction program was near completion and because most Northerners seemed to give it general approval. It was still possible that a majority of the Republicans, as well as the Democrats, might be won over to his program, or at least to a modified version of it.

Even after Johnson began organizing governments in the southern states, most Republicans had shown considerable reluctance to break with him. In June 1865, Carl Schurz, while urging Johnson to commit himself to Negro suffrage, begged Sumner not to repudiate the President. In August, John Murray Forbes, a radical Bostonian, wrote: "My great hope lies in Pres. Johnson's stubborn democracy. I have full faith in his hatred of the slave aristocracy; and if he finds that under his experiment the oligarchy rears its head and begins to grasp the reins of power, I look to see him promptly resume the military power."

---

[1] Perhaps a fifth group, labeled "moderate radicals," should be added. This would be the most accurate way to identify a number of important Congressmen, among them Senators William Pitt Fessenden of Maine and Lyman Trumbull of Illinois.

IV: *Triumph of the Radicals*

Many Republicans, like Forbes, referred to Johnson's program as an "experiment," and for a long time they hoped that he would see his mistake and abandon it. "Nobody approves it," Senator Lot M. Morrill of Maine assured Sumner. "Still it is only an experiment—let him try it." *Harper's Weekly* was confident that Johnson was merely "feeling his way," that he did "not assume to dictate in any least degree to Congress." As late as February 1866, a caucus of Ohio Republican state legislators, still seeking harmony, resolved that Johnson had "wisely inaugurated the necessary measures of reconstruction" but that only Congress could complete the process. They urged both President and Congress to "waive extreme opinions . . . and harmoniously provide . . . moderate but effectual measures of a lasting reconstruction."

Gradually the Republicans became more sarcastic in their references to Johnson's "experiment," but before Congress assembled only a few of them had given up on him completely. Stevens, Sumner, and Wade had lost faith by the summer of 1865. In July, Wade had written: "We have in truth already lost the whole moral effect of our victories over the rebellion, and the golden opportunity for humiliating and destroying the influence of the Southern aristocracy has gone forever."

The moderates, however, were still hopeful that conflict between Congress and the President could be avoided. To win them—and thus a majority in Congress—Johnson would have had to be prudent and flexible, while those who controlled his governments in the South would have had to use some discretion. Instead, the President's tactless, uncompromising, and violent behavior, and the southern politicians' indifference to northern public opinion, eventually forced the moderates into an alliance with the radicals. Consequently, by the summer of 1866 the radicals, with their new recruits, had control of Congress and were finally in a position to assume the direction of reconstruction themselves.

For more than two years, from the convening of Congress in December 1865 to the President's impeachment trial in the spring of 1868, the radicals and the Johnsonians engaged in a fascinating dialogue. Some of the dialogue, to be sure, was shrill and irresponsible—a mere exchange of insults and false accusations. But much of it was an intensely serious discussion of several fundamental problems: the proper relationship of the legislative and executive branches, the legitimate areas of federal and state responsibility, and the terms that might justly be imposed upon the defeated South.

Often the dialogue involved vaguely defined constitutional issues, especially the abstract question of whether the southern states had or had not ever been out of the federal Union. Contrary to Johnson's contention that these states never had been out and therefore needed only the restoration of loyal governments, the radicals argued that by trying to secede they had destroyed the old political relationship. Thaddeus Stevens maintained that they had in fact seceded, that during the war they had been given belligerent rights, and that they were now conquered provinces "subject to all the liabilities of a vanquished foe." Congress alone had the power to rebuild the southern states "and to admit them into the Union, if they should be judged fit to resume the privileges which they renounced and sought to destroy." Charles Sumner, taking a somewhat more moderate position, denied that the southern states ever had seceded; instead, by their acts of rebellion, they had committed suicide and reverted to the condition of territories. They were now subject to such rules and regulations as Congress might prescribe, and they could not regain their statehood until Congress was ready to give it to them. George W. Julian explained what these radical theories were going to mean in practice: the rebel states would be treated "as outside of their constitutional relations to the Union, and as incapable of restoring themselves to it except on conditions to be prescribed by Congress."

On both sides, however, the central issue of the dialogue was the place of the free Negro in American society. This was the question that the radicals and Johnsonians always came to sooner or later. Between them they gave shape to the debate—its terms, its form, its assumptions—that has raged with varying degrees of intensity ever since.

When the Negro was the subject of the dialogue, President Johnson ranged himself on the side of the racists and, in effect, demanded that the South remain a "white man's country." In his third annual message he told Congress that the Negroes were entitled to be "well and humanely governed" and to be protected in their rights of person and property. But, he added, "it must be acknowledged that in the progress of nations negroes have shown less capacity for government than any other race of people. No independent government of any form has ever been successful in their hands. On the contrary, wherever they have been left to their own devices they have shown a constant tendency to relapse into barbarism. . . . The great difference between the two races in physical, mental, and moral characteristics will prevent an amalgamation or fusion of them together in one homogeneous mass. . . . Of all the dangers which our nation has yet encountered, none are equal to those which must result from the success of the effort now making to Africanize the [southern] half of our country."

The rebuttal came from the radicals of the reconstruction era: "This is not a 'white man's government,' " said

Thaddeus Stevens. "To say so is political blasphemy, for it violates the fundamental principles of our gospel of liberty. This is man's government; the government of all men alike." The goal of reconstruction, Stevens maintained, was to give Negroes perfect equality before the law and "to overcome the prejudice and ignorance and wickedness which resisted such reform." The South, said Charles Sumner, must be reconstructed in accordance with the principles of the Declaration of Independence, with government founded upon the consent of the governed. "If all whites must vote, then must all blacks." And, added Senator Henry Wilson, "we must see to it that the man made free by the Constitution . . . is a freeman indeed; that he can go where he pleases, work when and for whom he pleases; that he can sue and be sued; that he can lease and buy and sell and own property, real and personal; that he can go into the schools and educate himself and his children; that the rights and guarantees of the . . . common law are his, and that he walks the earth, proud and erect in the conscious dignity of a free man." Horace Greeley, in the New York *Tribune*, denounced the state laws that prohibited marriages between Negroes and whites and advocated their repeal.

Demands for racial equality such as these went far beyond what the average white man, North or South, was then ready to support. "I am no advocate for social equality," wrote Gideon Welles, "nor do I labor for political or civil equality with the negro. I do not want him at my table, nor do I care to have him in the jury box, or in the legislative hall, or on the bench." Early in 1866 several Ohio Republicans warned John Sherman that agitation for Negro suffrage would defeat the party in the fall elections. Another told him that many Republicans were "becoming vexed at this everlasting tinkering about the

Negroes." A Cincinnati Republican wrote sarcastically that "no disease has ever proven half so intractable as that called 'nigger on the brain.' " In their racial attitudes the radical Republicans were always a minority group, and it was only when they broadened their appeal—as the prewar abolitionists had done—that they managed for a time to win the general approval of the northern electorate.

Moreover, the conservative Johnsonians would never concede that the radicals were seriously concerned about the welfare of the Negro; nor would historians who wrote in the Dunning tradition. The radicals, they said, used the rhetoric of equality, natural rights, and democracy as a camouflage to conceal the sordid purposes that lay beneath their pretended idealism. The conservatives apparently could not believe that any sane white man would actually favor the equality of the races and make this a genuine reason for opposition to Johnson's plan of reconstruction. Men who professed such a motive were either unbalanced fanatics or liars. The Johnsonians relegated a few of the radicals to the first of these categories but most of them to the second. In short, the typical radical had no sincere interest in the Negro at all—only a desire to exploit him. The vindictive radical would elevate the Negro to punish the southern white man; the ambitious radical would enfranchise the Negro to use him as a political tool; and the venal radical would mislead the Negro to protect the interests of northern businessmen.[2]

These explanations of radical behavior introduce the

---

[2] The Fourteenth Amendment, said Senator Thomas A. Hendricks, "is a proposition, first, to perpetuate the rule and power of a political party; in the second place, it is a proposition the tendency of which is to place agriculture under the control and power of manufactures and commerce forever; and, in the third place, it is intended, I believe, as a punishment upon the southern States."

extremely subtle and elusive problem of motivation. In the cases of Lincoln and Johnson this subject is often dealt with as if it were really no problem at all. The two Presidents were above guile; they were incapable of thinking of reconstruction in terms of strategies; they had no secret motives. Lincoln asked for a swift and painless reconstruction program because he was without malice and overflowed with compassion. Johnson vetoed measures to protect southern Negroes because he respected the rights of the states and feared the expansion of federal power. This is what they said, and this is what they meant—and, indeed, there is no reason to doubt that what they said was, in part at least, what they meant. But the radicals apparently *never* said what they meant; they were always guided by the unarticulated motive—or nearly always, save for those rare moments of candor when the mask was briefly lifted. Those moments of truth, the Johnsonians believed, occurred when the radicals betrayed some sordid purpose, not when they described some noble goal. The conservatives seldom doubted their capacity to understand why the radicals would protect the Negroes and overturn the Johnson governments in the South. But in actual fact they were about as reliable interpreters of radical motivation as the radicals were of conservative motivation.

This is not to say that the Johnsonians were altogether wrong in their appraisal of the radicals—when, for example, they accused the radicals of vindictiveness. "Hate, revenge, and persecution enter largely into their composition," wrote Gideon Welles. "These fanatics want a God to punish, not to love, those who do not agree with them." Indeed, these men, who had just emerged from four years of war, did have in them a streak of hatred and bitterness toward the South, a desire to punish her for her "treason." Thaddeus Stevens, for one, vowed that he would devote the "small remnant" of his life to the "punishment of traitors." "A rebellion only less guilty than that of the devilish angels was waged with fiendish cruelty against the best Government on earth," he said. "Did any respectable Government ever before allow such high criminals to escape with such shameful impunity? . . . No, sir; they have not been punished as they deserve. They have exchanged forgiveness with the President, and been sent on their way rejoicing." Stevens had no sympathy for that "morbid sensibility, sometimes called mercy, which affects a few of all classes, from the priest to the clown, which has more sympathy for the murderer on the gallows than for his victim." He would execute only a few of the leading rebels, "but surely *some* victims must propitiate the names of our starved, murdered, slaughtered martyrs."

Stevens, in fact, is usually portrayed as the most venomous of the radicals, and amateur psychoanalysts have offered an intriguing variety of ways to explain him. Some have emphasized his unhappy childhood (his father, an alcoholic, deserted the family); some his club foot; some the fact that his Caledonia ironworks were destroyed when Lee invaded Pennsylvania; some the fact that he had a mulatto housekeeper who they assume was his mistress; and some his thwarted ambition—the fact that he failed to win a coveted Senate seat or Cabinet post. These various experiences doubtless helped to shape the personality of this sarcastic, crusty old bachelor and to instill in him a sense of grievance that was relieved by the punishment of others. But it is doubtful that revenge was more than a superficial explanation of Stevens's reconstruction goals; indeed, some of his more virulent invectives seem to be nothing more than deliberate rhetorical hyperbole.

The malice toward Southerners evident in Stevens's

speeches was matched by that which many rank-and-file Republicans expressed in letters to their Congressmen. An Indiana Republican praised Stevens for rebuking those "who call these Southern hounds 'our Southern brethren.' " "I beg of you to do what you can to have somebody convicted and hung and thereby 'make treason odious,' " a Cleveland Republican wrote Sherman. "It will be [an] everlasting disgrace to the nation if this is not done." Nor did the radical press waste much charity on rebels. The New York *Independent* recommended that Negro troops be used for an indefinite military occupation of the South. "They are the natural terriers to watch such rats. They know every trick of the rattlesnake; therefore let them be the chief charmers to tame it and draw its fangs."

Gideon Welles described a second motive of the radicals: political advantage. He was convinced that "intense partisanship" rather than philanthropy was at the root of the movement for Negro suffrage. Four fifths of the radicals, he wrote, "are small party men . . . without any knowledge of the science of government or of our Constitution. With them all the great, overpowering purpose and aim are office and patronage. Most of their legislation relates to office and their highest conception of legislative duty has in view place and how to get it."

Since Welles had himself spent many years in public life, one need not take at face value his seemingly naïve dismay at discovering that radical politicians were, after all, motivated at least in part by considerations of practical politics. For surely they did search for means to keep their party in power and to consolidate its position. By 1865, the Republican party was no longer a spontaneous grass-roots movement as it had been to some extent at the time of its birth in the 1850's. It had now become institutionalized; it was dominated by professional politicians;

and it had developed powerful political machines in the various northern states. Playing the political game according to a familiar set of rules, Republicans made the winning of elections and control of the patronage ends in themselves. And the radicals clearly believed that postponing the seating of southern Congressmen and repudiating the Johnson governments would serve these ends. Moderate as well as radical Republicans were afraid that southern and western agrarians might once more combine in the Democratic party, for this was the alliance that had dominated national politics most of the time in prewar years. Equally distressing was the fact that the South would now actually have greater power in the House of Representatives than it did before the war. When southern Negroes were slaves only three fifths of them were counted in the apportionment of Representatives; but with slavery abolished, they would all be counted, and southern representation would be increased by approximately fifteen. This, said the radicals bitterly, would be the South's reward for her treason!

The solution to this political dilemma, the radicals believed, was the enfranchisement of the Negroes and a vigorous campaign to win their votes for the Republican party. Thaddeus Stevens, who seemed to enjoy shocking the Johnsonians, once frankly admitted that he had a political motive. In a speech before the House of Representatives, he declared that Negro suffrage was necessary to insure the ascendancy of his party. "Do you avow the party purpose? exclaims some horror-stricken demagogue. I do. For I believe . . . that on the continued ascendancy of that party depends the safety of this great nation. If [Negro] suffrage is excluded in the rebel States then every one of them is sure to send a solid rebel representative delegation to Congress. . . . They, with their kindred

Copperheads of the North, would always elect the President and control Congress. . . . For these, among other reasons, I am for negro suffrage in every rebel State."[3]

To evaluate properly the political motive behind the radical program, one must remember that conservative Republicans thought in political terms as well. They simply came to different conclusions about how best to keep the Republican party in power. First, they were fearful that a break with Johnson would split the party and throw the government into the hands of the Democrats once more. Second, like Lincoln, they preferred to build their party in the South with the support of conservative whites, rather than on the basis of Negro suffrage. Third, they were convinced that Negro suffrage was unpopular in the North and that the party advocating it would be repudiated at the polls. Finally, they believed, as John Binny warned Stevens, that Negro voters "would be blind tools in the hands of their late masters. . . . Mr. Sumner expects those blacks to adhere to the Union party, but is there not reason to fear they would be gained over to the ex-rebel side?" In any case, an Ohio conservative advised John Sherman, the primary aim of Republican Congressmen should be to maintain party unity. "I am willing to sacrifice almost anything to keep the democratic party out of power." The welfare of the party, then, was a matter of concern to radical, moderate, and conservative Republicans alike.

The third motive of the radicals, according to the Johnsonians, was to protect the interests of their northern business allies. "These Radical patriots are swindling the

---

[3] In a private letter to F. A. Conkling, January 6, 1868, Stevens clarified his position: "I have never insisted that the franchise should be unjustly regulated so as to secure a Republican ascendancy but I have insisted and do insist that there can be no unjust regulation of that franchise which will give to any other party the power."

country while imposing on its credulity," wrote Welles. "The granting of acts of incorporation, bounties, special privileges, favors, and profligate legislation of every description is shocking." And, indeed, the Congress that repudiated the Johnson governments in the South did devote much of its time to economic legislation: to tariff laws in support of iron and wool manufacturers; to various proposals for direct or indirect subsidizing of commercial interests; to measures beneficial to railroad builders; and to policies that would protect investors in national banks and government securities. The Republican party had become, in part, the political agency of the northern middle classes and of northern business enterprise. The postwar era was the time of the Great Barbecue, when the federal government, under Republican control, generously turned the nation's natural resources over to individuals and corporations for private exploitation. But the agrarian interests in the South and West, ever suspicious of bankers, capitalists, and urban entrepreneurs generally, posed a serious threat to the economic groups the Republican party represented and to the legislation passed for their benefit.

The radical refusal to recognize the Johnson governments and the demand for Negro suffrage were doubtless related to these practical matters. Thaddeus Stevens was himself an iron manufacturer, a firm ally of Pennsylvania's iron interests, and closely associated with the directors and lobbyists of the Northern Pacific and Pennsylvania railroads. Senator Chandler was a wealthy Detroit merchant. Senator Roscoe Conkling of New York was a corporation lawyer identified with bankers and railroad financiers. Senator Wade was the friend of western manufacturers and wool growers. Even Sumner, though no favorite of the business community of his state, was a conscientious protector of the textile industry and of the investors in government securities.

When on rare occasions the radicals publicly associated their reconstruction program with economic policy, they usually stressed the tariff and the national debt incurred during the Civil War. Without Negro suffrage, warned Stevens, Northerners would be "the perpetual vassals of the free-trade . . . South." Combine the southern vote with the northern Copperhead vote, said John Murray Forbes, "and you have a party strong enough to deliberately destroy the credit of our government by repudiation." Another radical declared that the Southerners whom Johnson wanted Congress to seat had as their goal "a great reduction of the Tariff . . . perhaps Free Trade to culminate with Repudiation [of the public debt] . . . and how sweet and complete will be the revenge of . . . [the rebels] if they can ruin the North by Free Trade and Repudiation." Senator Conkling asked his business friends whether they were ready to sacrifice their interests to the alliance of rebels and Copperheads. "What would become of the public debt and the public credit? . . . Are you ready to put your rights, your property and the honor of the nation to be raffled for by the . . . betrayers of your country?" Sumner insisted that only through Negro suffrage "can you save the national debt from the inevitable repudiation which awaits it when recent rebels in conjunction with northern . . . [Democrats] once more bear sway. . . . [The Negro] is our best guarantee. Use him." Elizur Wright spelled out the radical economic motive in remarkably specific terms: "I could easily convince any man, who does not allow his prejudices to stand in the way of his interests, that it will probably make a difference of at least $1,000,000,000 in the development of the national debt, whether we reconstruct on the basis of loyal white and black votes, or on white votes exclusively, and that he can better afford to give the Government at least one-quarter of his estate than to have it try the latter experiment." Many radicals declared that the South would have to be settled by northern men, developed with northern capital, and indoctrinated with northern views on economic policy—in short, "northernized"—before it could be trusted with political power once more.

By 1866, after an initial inclination to favor Johnson's reconstruction plan, most northern bankers, manufacturers, and bondholders gravitated toward the radicals. Thus was sealed, said the Johnsonians, an unholy alliance between seekers after vengeance, cynical political opportunists, and greedy capitalists.

The Johnsonians and historians who wrote in the Dunning tradition thus demonstrated with abundant evidence that the radicals were something less than saints and that some of their motives were ignoble. But this leaves several aspects of the problem of radical motivation still unexplored. In the first place, even if one were to assume that radical motivation was entirely sordid, it does not necessarily follow that their program itself was reprehensible. Since their program included the granting of citizenship, civil rights, and the ballot to American Negroes, it may be that we are here confronted with a group which pursued objectives that were morally good for reasons that were morally bad. If that is the case, the historian will have to decide which has the greater historical significance: the praiseworthy program or the ignominious motive. He may, in fact, have to expand the classic moral dilemma of means and ends to means, *motives,* and ends.

But this is only part of the problem. For, as we have seen, the radicals in their public utterances, only rarely betrayed an unidealistic motive. Even Thad Stevens, while demanding Negro suffrage in order to punish the South, strengthen the Republicans, and save the protective tariff, also made some noble statements about the rights to which American Negroes were entitled. "Every man," he said, "no matter what his race or color . . . has an equal right to justice, honesty, and fair play with every other man; and the law should secure him those rights. The same law which condemns or acquits an African should condemn or acquit a white man. The same law which gives a verdict in a white man's favor should give a verdict in a black man's favor on the same state of facts. Such is the law of God and such ought to be the law of man." This was the characteristic tone of radical speeches when the subject of Negro rights arose. But the Johnsonians did not believe the radicals when they spoke in this fashion, only when they spoke of using the Negroes for their own selfish purposes. The Johnsonians, in short, accused the radicals of conscious hypocrisy.

This accusation, of course, was based upon an assumed ability to read the minds and hearts of the radicals. It was also based upon some rather dubious psychology, for man's hypocrisy is not usually at the conscious level. Few men possess the self-understanding, few are capable of the deliberate cynicism, that would enable them knowingly to deceive others about their motives. Given man's capacity for self-deception and self-justification, it is doubtful that many of the radicals were conscious hypocrites. Given the politician's tendency to identify the welfare of his country with the welfare of his party—of which there is no better example than Thad Stevens—it may well be that the radicals had persuaded themselves that what was good for the Republican party was good for everyone.

But the most important question is whether the radicals, as the Johnsonians believed, were almost never motivated by genuine idealism. Were their rare confessions of dishonorable purposes the only occasions when they spoke the truth? Were their far more numerous professions of exalted motives just so much sham? Assuming that men in public life normally display at least a modicum of honesty and decency along with their presumed penchant for sly strategy, is there evidence to suggest that the radicals were below average in this respect? In answering these questions one ought not pretend to have read the minds of the radicals more successfully than the Johnsonians did, or to know the precise mixture of base and noble motives that underlay their reconstruction plans. But when a substantial body of men are accused of more than normal moral corruption, the burden of proof is on the accusers. As a matter of fact, such evidence does not exist; instead, there are a number of circumstances that suggest quite the opposite conclusion.

Back in the 1850's, when the Republican party was organized, a variety of groups were attracted to it. Among them were men who had been active in the reform movements, including abolitionism, that had flourished in the 1830's and 1840's. As heirs of the Enlightenment, these reformers believed in the doctrine of natural rights and in the equality of all men before the law and in the sight of God. Influenced by the romantic movement of the early nineteenth century, they had a transcendental faith in the essential goodness of man, in his ultimate perfectibility, and in his capacity to know truth intuitively. As nineteenth-century liberals, they believed in the autonomous individual—his right to control his own destiny—and therefore regarded slavery as the ultimate abomination. Moreover, they had an overpowering sense of personal guilt for the survival of evils such as slavery, and of duty

99

to work for their eradication. They joined the Republican party in order to make it a political agency of moral reform, especially to convert it into an instrument of the antislavery crusade. Even in the 1850's the reformers were sometimes called radical Republicans; and though they were in a minority in the new party, they were the custodians of its conscience. Without them the party would have had no distinctive identity—it would have been, as one radical said, *"Hamlet* with Hamlet left out."

The radicals had great influence at the first Republican national nominating convention in 1856, when the party platform reaffirmed the principles of the Declaration of Independence, denounced slavery as a "relic of barbarism," and demanded that Congress exclude slavery from all new states and territories. During the next four years, the radicals opposed efforts to soften the platform of 1856 and to give greater emphasis to such mundane issues as the tariff, banking, and internal improvements. In 1860, they threatened to quit the party if it betrayed its antislavery principles; one radical described the new platform and the moderate Lincoln as representing a "superficial and only half-developed Republicanism." His strategy in that campaign was to *"assume* the whole movement to be antislavery, and *on that account* call on men to support it, and if any man fails, after election hold him up as an apostate from the faith."

During the secession crisis following Lincoln's election, the radicals, by threatening again to desert the Republicans, played a crucial role in defeating those who urged compromise with the South. "I helped to make the Republican party," vowed an Illinois radical, "and if it forsakes its distinctive ideas, I can help to tear it down, and help to erect a new party that shall never cower to any slave driver." James Russell Lowell advised Republicans to stand firm, reminding them that "material prosperity was never known to abide long in a country that had lost its political morality. . . . It is time that the North should learn that it has nothing left to compromise but the rest of its self-respect."

When Civil War followed, the radicals had no doubt about its fundamental cause. It was, they said, the result of a "blasphemous attempt to rear an empire on the corner-stone of human slavery"; hence there could be no domestic peace until slavery was abolished. To fight without this goal, argued Wendell Phillips, was to wage "a murderous and wasteful war . . . for no purpose at all." The moral fervor which radicals injected into the war, as well as the logic of events, eventually transformed what began as a struggle to preserve the Union into a crusade for freedom. Among their victories the radicals counted the Confiscation Acts, the Emancipation Proclamation, the decision in 1863 to accept Negro recruits in the Union Army, and, finally, the Thirteenth Amendment. In short, much of the nobility of the Civil War years, and most of the idealism of the Union cause, were supplied by the radical Republicans.

This being the case, it would be difficult to explain why their idealism suddenly should have died in 1865, when they turned against Johnson and demanded that Negro freedom be given federal support. The radicals of the reconstruction era were either the reformers of the prewar years or men who had been strongly influenced by their moral imperatives. In fact, radical reconstruction ought to be viewed in part as the last great crusade of the nine-teenth-century romantic reformers. Since the radicals were in politics, we may assume that they had learned to accommodate themselves to some of the practical realities of public life and that their pristine innocence may have eroded in the passing years. Nevertheless, it is likely that the radicals were, if anything, somewhat *less* opportunistic in their purposes and a little *more* candid in their public utterances than the average American politician has been. Their pleas for justice for the Negro, their objection to the Johnson governments on the ground that the Black Codes were restoring a form of slavery, cannot be discounted as pure hypocrisy. To the practical motives that the radicals occasionally revealed must be added the moral idealism that they inherited from the abolitionists.

The radical George W. Julian of Indiana, for example, was lecturing his fellow Republicans, not bidding for their votes, when he said to them: "The real trouble is that *we hate the negro*. It is not his ignorance that offends us, but his color. . . . [Let] one rule be adopted for white and black, and let us, if possible, dispossess our minds, utterly, of the vile spirit of caste which has brought upon our country all its woes." Senator Henry Wilson of Massachusetts could hardly have pleased the white workingmen of his state, among whom there was much race prejudice, when he drew no distinction between them and Negro workers. "We have advocated the rights of the black man, he said, "because the black man was the most oppressed type of the toiling men of this country. . . . The man who is the enemy of the black laboring man is the enemy of the white laboring man the world over. The same influences that go to keep down and crush down the rights of the poor black man bear down and oppress the poor white laboring man."

In the case of Senator Charles Sumner, to deny the reality of his moral fervor and humanitarian idealism is to deny the reality of the man himself. Sumner could on occasion act expediently to hold his seat in the Senate, but in no sense was he the shrewd, scheming politician, the adroit party manager. Rather, he used his prestige in the Senate to lecture his colleagues on their duties and on the penalties for betraying eternal principles. Before the Civil War Sumner had ardently supported numerous reform movements: world peace, temperance, women's rights, prison reform, and, of course, abolitionism. Now, with a similar devotion to the radical cause, he demanded civil and political rights for Negroes. On the subject of human rights he would hear of no compromises: "I had hoped that the day of compromise with wrong had passed forever. Ample experience shows that it is the least practical mode of settling questions involving moral principles. A moral principle cannot be compromised." But even the Johnsonians agreed that Sumner was probably less a hypocrite than a fanatic—a man "of good intentions," Claude Bowers wrote, "given to the making of great blunders."[4]

Thaddeus Stevens, a vastly more complicated personality than Sumner, had an overpowering political ambition and was a faithful servant of manufacturing and railroad interests. He was hardly the Great Commoner, the persistent and consistent champion of the common man, as one of his biographers describes him. Yet in Pennsylvania politics he had battled for a system of free public education and the prevention of the disenfranchisement of the Negroes. Now he was a leader in the postwar struggle for Negro rights. "I care not what you may say of Negro equality," he told his constituents, "I care not what you may say of radicalism; these are my principles, and with the help of God I shall die with them." He demanded "a radical reorganization in southern institutions, habits and manners. . . . This may startle feeble minds and shake weak nerves. So do all great improvements in the political and moral world. It requires a heavy impetus to drive for-

---

[4] Bowers, *The Tragic Era*, p. 335.

ward a sluggish people. When it was first proposed to free the slaves, and arm the blacks, did not half the nation tremble? The prim conservatives, the snobs, and the male waiting-maids in Congress, were in hysterics." When Stevens died, his will provided that he was to be buried in a Negro cemetery in protest against the exclusion of Negroes from the burial grounds of the whites. It would, therefore, be difficult to understand him without giving some credence to these external manifestations of moral conviction.

Indeed, few of the radicals can be understood unless they are linked with the antislavery crusade, for that was the source of some of their goals and much of their rhetoric. Like the abolitionists they spoke of regenerating the South, of sacred duties, of the will of God, and of the evils of compromise. *"Absolute right* must prevail," wrote a Chicago radical, " 'tis demanded by God, and the spirit of the people." A Cleveland radical told John Sherman that his greatest fear came from the signs of timidity among certain Republican leaders, "for the moment we begin to trim and relax from the great principles of equal rights and justice to all, that moment there is danger. The difference between the two parties will become less and less apparent, and the result will be as inevitable as the fate of the old Whig party." Edwin L. Godkin preached to the politicians incessantly on the moral issues of the day through the columns of the New York *Nation*. The freedmen of the South, he wrote, "are a part of the American commonwealth; and we seek their education, elevation, and happiness not simply from pity, but because we believe the continued degradation of any portion of its people to be dangerous to the state and a scandal to free government." To accept the doctrine that this is a white man's government "will make the very name of

IV: *Triumph of the Radicals*

American democracy a hissing and a byword amongst all the nations of the earth." A Rhode Island Republican who confessed that he shared somewhat the "common prejudice" against Negroes, still asked "that our country shall do something to repay the immense debt we owe them. I cannot but feel that it was their fervent prayers and strong arms that signally helped save our Union in the hour of deepest peril." A genuine desire to do justice to the Negro, then, was one of the mainsprings of radicalism.

With this thread of idealism in mind, it is necessary to examine once more the radicals' alleged economic motive —their supposed identification with northern capitalist interests. Those who gave radical reconstruction an economic interpretation were often guilty of several oversimplifications. In the first place, they overlooked the fact that there was no clear division over questions of economic policy between Lincoln and the conservative Republicans on the one hand and the radical Republicans on the other. Lincoln favored the tariff, a national banking system, federal subsidies to the railroads, and federal appropriations for internal improvements; and he signed every measure for these purposes that Congress passed. Though President Johnson disapproved of these policies, the conservative Republicans who supported his reconstruction program usually did not. This is why Johnson made almost no attempt to stress economic issues in the congressional elections of 1866.

In addition, the economic interpretation is based on the assumption that the northern business community was united to promote a common economic program, whereas no such unity ever really existed. Iron and steel manufacturers favored high tariffs, but the railroad builders and shipping interests wanted the tariffs reduced. Wool manufacturers were protectionists—provided the duty on raw wool was not raised too high. Bondholders and most bankers (not all) demanded a quick return to the gold standard; but manufacturers, seeking capital for expansion, usually favored a moderate paper-money inflation. Divisions such as these troubled the radicals in Congress, too. For example, Thad Stevens favored high tariffs and inflation, as did his industrialist friends in Pennsylvania; while Charles Sumner favored tariff reduction and the gold standard. This does not mean that none of the radical Republicans were serving northern business interests, or that as a group they lacked economic motives. But it does discredit the idea of a vast conspiracy between the radical phalanx and a solid corps of capitalists to use reconstruction and Negro rights as a smokescreen to conceal a carefully planned program of economic aggrandizement.

Still another oversimplification of those who gave radical reconstruction an economic interpretation stems from their underlying conception of what is real and what is unreal in human affairs. When they discovered an economic motive, they seemed to feel that they were dealing with reality—with something that reflects the true nature of man. But when they were confronted with moral arguments, they seemed to feel that they were dealing with something that is slightly fraudulent, and they began searching for hidden meanings. This rather cavalier dismissal of man's moral and humanitarian impulses betrays not only a cynical but a superficial understanding of human behavior. As a matter of fact, for a few of the radicals —Sumner, for example—we might be nearer the truth if we stood the economic interpretation on its head. Sumner was probably revealing his *true* motive when he spoke in terms of moral principles. And when he argued that Negro suffrage was necessary to prevent a repudiation of the public debt, he may *then* have had a concealed motive—that is, he may have believed that this was the way to convert bondholders to his moral principles.[5] In that case it would be the economic argument that was slightly fraudulent and had a hidden meaning.

Finally, insofar as the radicals were economically motivated, we cannot assume that their efforts to aid business enterprise were wholly devoid of a certain kind of idealism. For if economics is the Dismal Science, it is nevertheless often pursued with considerable moral passion. To be sure, one may question the wisdom of some of the fiscal measures that Congress passed during the reconstruction years; many of the radicals were blind to the abuses of the totally undisciplined and irresponsible businessmen of their day; and few of them could resist altogether the enticements of the Great Barbecue. But as far as motives are concerned, the important question is whether the radicals, through their economic program—to the extent that they had one—were consciously plotting to bring about socially undesirable results. By way of a partial answer, this much can be said at least: there is little in their public or private papers to indicate that this was the case, and much to suggest that such injuries to the public as occurred had been neither planned nor anticipated.

Most of the radicals who were committed to a high tariff, the national banking system, and subsidies to the railroads seemed to believe quite sincerely that these measures were designed to benefit and enrich not just special interest groups but the country as a whole. Public lands and mineral and timber resources could almost be given away to private entrepreneurs, because there was a general belief then that America's resources were inexhaustible and that this was the best way to put them to productive use.

---

[5] He also believed that repaying the bondholders was itself based on a high moral principle.

In this society of free farmers and growing industries, every man was presumed to have an equal chance for material success. With the abolition of slavery American labor had escaped a serious threat; and now, if the southern planters were crushed, the last vestige of an American aristocracy would be destroyed. "Strip a proud nobility of their bloated estates," said Stevens, "reduce them to a level with plain Republicans; send them forth to labor, and teach their children to enter the workshops or handle the plow." Meanwhile, he advised his countrymen, build the railroads, bring in immigrants to settle the West, encourage manufacturing, and all will prosper. Some complain, said Senator Wade, "that eastern manufacturers grow rich by manufacturing. I hope they do; and I hope . . . that we of the Northwest will have the sense and sagacity to make use of the same means to enrich ourselves."

The historian Matthew Josephson aptly described the economic idealism in the radical program. The views of these politicians, he wrote, had been "colored by the whole social order from which they sprang. . . . Instinctively they had learned to admire the thrifty, workaday, progressive ways of their own industrialists, artisans, and free farmers . . . and to loathe the economic backwardness . . . of the [South]." To men like Thad Stevens, "new railroads, new factories and foundries, all the busy, profitable industry of the North, were linked with the grand march of humanity toward a more productive and fuller life, while the world of the Southern plantation embodied the ways of sloth, backwardness, and darkness itself."[6]

These, then, were the practical and idealistic motives of the radical Republicans; for these reasons the Civil War had been fought and the South vanquished. But now, said the radicals, President Johnson, through his plan of recon-

[6] Matthew Josephson: *The Politicos* (New York, 1938), pp. 18–19, 48.

struction, threatened to deprive the North of the fruits of its costly victory. The fear of a revival of the southern rebellion, the desire to avoid having to fight the war over again, were crucial factors in determining northern postwar attitudes toward the South. "What we want, and what is our due, is indemnity for the past and security for the future," wrote a Vermont Republican. Schurz recalled that Northerners "asked themselves quite seriously whether there was not real danger that the legitimate results of the war, for the achievement of which they had sacrificed uncounted thousands of lives and the fruits of many, many years of labor, were not in grave jeopardy again. Their alarm was not artificially produced by political agitation. It was sincere and profound and began to grow angry." Indeed, this desire to preserve the fruits of victory, which has always helped to shape the immediate postwar policies of the victor toward the vanquished, was doubtless a major reason for northern support of radical reconstruction. In the words of a shrewd young contemporary French newspaperman, Georges Clemenceau: "When anyone has for four successive years joined in such a struggle as that which the United States has seen . . . [he desires] not to lose the dearly bought fruits of so many painful sacrifices. When the war ended, the North was concerned not to let itself be tricked out of what it had spent so much trouble and perseverance to win."

For the South to have gained almost immediate autonomy in its domestic affairs, as it would have under Johnson's program, would have required of its leaders extraordinary restraint, a quality for which they had not been distinguished in recent years. One of the radicals found consolation in this fact. In prewar years, he recalled, "whenever all looked gloomy for our cause, something of outrage or extravagant pretensions has been put forth on the part of the South which has brought our people to their senses." Now he expected—indeed hoped—that Southerners would "behave so outrageously as to awaken . . . the North once more." And the South obliged with its Black Codes, with major race riots in Memphis and New Orleans and smaller ones elsewhere, and by electing many distinguished Confederates to offices in the Johnson governments.

All this was ammunition for the radicals, and with it they soon put the Johnsonians to rout. On the first day that Congress met, the radicals and moderates united to prevent the seating of Senators and Representatives from the eleven states that had formed the Confederacy; in this manner they prevented, at least temporarily, congressional recognition of the Johnson governments. The following February they agreed that no Congressmen from any southern state should be seated in either house until both had "declared such state entitled to such representation."

In December the radicals and moderates also agreed to establish a Joint Committee on Reconstruction to investigate conditions in the South, to receive all bills and resolutions relating to reconstruction, and eventually to make such recommendations to Congress as it thought appropriate. The committee consisted of six members from the Senate and nine from the House, of whom twelve were Republicans and three Democrats. Some of the leading radicals served on the committee, but the moderates actually controlled it, with Senator William Pitt Fessenden of Maine serving as chairman.[7] Fessenden justified the crea-

---

[7] The remaining members were Senators J. W. Grimes (Ia.), Ira Harris (N.Y.), J. M. Howard (Mich.), Reverdy Johnson (Md.), G. H. Williams (Ore.) ; and Representatives J. A. Bingham (Ohio), H. T. Blow (Mo.), G. S. Boutwell (Mass.), Roscoe Conkling (N.Y.), Henry Grider (Ky.), J. S. Morrill (Vt.), A. J. Rogers (N.J.), Thaddeus Stevens (Pa.), and E. B. Washburne (Ill.). Sumner was not appointed to the committee, though he wanted to serve.

tion of the committee not as a repudiation of Johnson but because the question of reconstruction was "of infinite importance, requiring calm and serious consideration." That Congress should give it such consideration "was not only wise in itself, but an imperative duty resting upon the representatives of the people."

On April 28, 1866, after meeting almost daily since the previous December, and after collecting volumes of testimony from witnesses residing in the South, the Joint Committee made its report. At the end of the war, the report declared, the rebellious states were "disorganized communities without civil governments." Elections held under these conditions could not be accepted as valid. Moreover, said the report, these states ought not to participate in the government of the country until the civil rights of all their citizens were secured and until the leaders of the rebellion had been excluded from public offices. The rebellion was suppressed by the people acting through the co-ordinate branches of the government, not by the President alone; hence the President did not have exclusive power to lay down the terms of a settlement. The report concluded that these states then lacked constituencies qualified to elect Senators and Representatives, that the majority of Southerners were still bitterly hostile to the government of the United States, and that the South therefore was not entitled to representation in Congress.

Meanwhile, President Johnson had strengthened the radical position by vetoing two congressional measures to protect southern Negroes that moderate Republicans believed he should have signed. The first, adopted in February 1866, extended the life and increased the powers of the Freedmen's Bureau, a wartime agency established to give assistance to the Negroes. The second, adopted the following month, was entitled "An act to protect all persons in the United States in their civil rights, and furnish the means of their vindication."[8] Johnson vetoed them even though most members of his Cabinet urged him to sign and, more important, even though the moderates made it clear that these measures were their minimum terms for continued support of the administration. Indeed, Johnson, in his veto messages, took such narrow constitutional grounds as to rule out not only these but almost any other steps to provide federal protection for the freedmen. An agency such as the Freedmen's Bureau, "for the support of indigent persons in the United States," he said, "was never contemplated by the authors of the Constitution." As for the Civil Rights bill, he argued rather lamely that it provided the Negro with "safeguards which go infinitely beyond any that the General Government has ever provided for the white race. In fact, the distinction of race and color is by the bill made to operate in favor of the colored and against the white race." Again the radicals and moderates united to pass the Civil Rights bill and a revised version of the Freedmen's Bureau bill over the President's vetoes, the first on April 9, the second on July 16, 1866.

On Washington's birthday, a few days after his veto of the Freedmen's Bureau bill, Johnson made a speech to a crowd of serenaders that had come to the White House grounds to pay their respects. Here he was at his tactless worst; and as he spoke, the years seemed to fall away and he was back on the stump in East Tennessee. He referred to the Joint Committee on Reconstruction as "an irresponsible central directory" that was usurping the powers of government, and he hinted darkly that the radicals were trying to dispose of him by assassination. "I fought traitors and treason in the South," he cried, "now when I turn

---

[8] For a discussion of these measures see Chapter Five.

around, and at the other end of the line find men—I care not by what name you call them—who will stand opposed to the restoration of the Union of these States, I am free to say to you that I am still in the field." Johnson's hint that there were traitors in the North brought a cry from the crowd for him to name them, and he responded: "You ask me who they are? I say Thaddeus Stevens of Pennsylvania is one; I say Mr. Sumner of the Senate is another; and Wendell Phillips is another."

These arrogant and intemperate remarks, together with the vetoes, made the break between Johnson and Congress all but final. Senator Wade reminded his colleagues that this "accidental Executive . . . was no more infallible than the rest of us poor mortals." Everywhere moderate Republicans expressed their disillusionment with the President and moved closer to the radicals. "Diversity of opinion is rapidly disappearing," an Ohio legislator wrote Senator John Sherman. "It is not now so much a difference of opinion as to whether we will or will not support Johnson but as to how we shall deprive his evident defection of its power of mischief."

If a last straw had been needed to complete the alienation of the moderates from the administration, Johnson provided it in his reaction to the Fourteenth Amendment which passed Congress in June.[9] An amendment, of course does not require the signature of the President, but Johnson nevertheless publicly denounced it and urged the southern states not to ratify it. Ten of the eleven former Confederate states took Johnson's advice, and their legislatures rejected the amendment, three of them unanimously, the rest with only a scattering of favorable votes. "If the constitutional amendment is adopted," Governor James L. Orr advised the South Carolina legislature, "let

---

[9] For an analysis of its provisions, see Chapter Five.

it be done by the irresponsible power of numbers, and let us preserve our self-respect, and the respect of our posterity, by refusing to be the mean instrument of our shame." Tennessee, however, ratified the amendment in July, and Congress quickly agreed to seat Senators and Representatives from that state once more. When the radical Unionist Governor William G. Brownlow notified the Senate that Tennessee had ratified, his telegram concluded: "Give my respects to the dead dog in the White House."

This increasingly bitter conflict set the tone for the wild political campaign that preceded the congressional elections of 1866. From late August to mid-September, Johnson went on a speaking tour that carried him as far west as Chicago and St. Louis; he was convinced that he needed merely to carry his message to "the people" to win their support. But his "swing around the circle" was a disaster for him and for the conservative cause. His speeches were, as Gideon Welles described them, "essentially but one speech often repeated"—they were rambling, vulgar, vindictive, and loaded with self-pity. In Cleveland he denounced Congress as "factious, domineering, tyrannical." When urged to hang Jefferson Davis, he retorted: "Why don't you hang Thad. Stevens and Wendell Phillips? I can tell you, my countrymen, I have been fighting traitors in the south, and . . . I am prepared to fight traitors at the north, God being willing with your help." The following passage from his Cleveland speech shows him at his worst:

> I care not for malignity. There is a certain portion of our countrymen that will respect their fellow-citizen whenever he is entitled to respect, and there is another portion that have no respect for themselves, and consequently have none for anybody else. I know a gentleman when I see him. And furthermore, I know when I look a man in the face—[Voice, "Which you can't do."]

I wish I could see you; I will bet now, if there could be a light reflected upon your face, that cowardice and treachery could be seen in it. Show yourself. Come out here where we can see you. If ever you shoot a man, you will stand in the dark and pull your trigger. I understand traitors; I have been fighting them for five years. We fought it out on the southern end of the line; now we are fighting in the other direction. And those men—such a one as insulted me to-night—you may say, has ceased to be a man, and in ceasing to be a man shrunk into the denomination of a reptile, and having so shrunken, as an honest man, I tread on him. I came here to-night not to criminate or recriminate, but when provoked my nature is not to advance but to defend, and when encroached upon, I care not from what quarter it comes, it will find resistance, and resistance at the threshold.

Johnson's friends were mortified that the President, as Henry J. Raymond wrote in the New York *Times,* "did not care about his dignity." He cannot, added Raymond, "enter upon an exchange of epithets with the brawling of a mob, without seriously compromising his official character and hazarding interests too momentous to be thus lightly imperiled." The country had never seen "so melancholy a spectacle" commented *Harper's Weekly.* Johnson had simply lost control of himself, and it is hardly surprising that some of the radicals in Congress should have begun to speak of impeachment.

Most of Johnson's political support now came from the Democrats, and throughout the campaign their central appeal was to the race prejudice of northern voters. Early in the campaign Thaddeus Stevens accurately predicted: "We shall hear repeated, ten thousand times, the cry of 'Negro Equality!' The radicals would thrust the negro into your parlors, your bedrooms, and the bosoms of your wives and daughters. . . . And then they will send up the grand chorus from every foul throat, 'nigger,' 'nigger,' 'nigger!' 'Down with the nigger party, we're for the white man's party.' " In September, when the Republicans held a convention of "Northern and Southern Loyalists" in Philadelphia, Frederick Douglass, the Negro abolitionist, attended as a delegate from Rochester and walked into the meeting arm-in-arm with the radical Theodore Tilton. The Democratic press ran headlines such as these: "First Grand National Convention of Negro Worshipers, Free Lovers, Spiritualists, and Negro Equality Men"; "Philadelphia Full of Miscegenationists"; and "Black and White Convention." The Republicans, said the Johnsonians, planned not only to Africanize the South but to pauperize northern white workingmen by encouraging the migration of cheap Negro labor. According to Frank Blair, a leader of the pro-Johnson forces in Missouri, it was also a "settled policy" of the Republicans to organize a regular army of Negro troops "which should give law to the country."

But the Republicans were at least as rugged campaigners as the Johnsonians. No charge against Johnson seemed too outrageous to make: he was a drunkard[1]; he was a rake and kept a harem in the White House; he was implicated in the assassination of Lincoln; he was a traitor plotting to turn the government over to southern rebels and northern Copperheads. Moreover, it was in this campaign that the Republicans developed their own variety of demagoguery, called "waving the bloody shirt," to match the racial dem-

---

[1] At the time of his inauguration as Vice President, Johnson had been ill and drank some whiskey to give him strength for the occasion. The whiskey made him drunk, and he made rather a disgrace of himself. The Democrats then accused him of being a drunkard—a charge the Republicans vigorously denied. In 1866, however, the Democrats defended him, while Republicans called him "the drunken tailor." There is, in fact, no evidence that Johnson drank excessively.

agoguery of the Democrats. Throughout the campaign Republican orators strove to keep alive the passions of the war years, to link the Democratic party with treason and the Republican party with patriotism. Governor Oliver P. Morton of Indiana gave a classic statement of the bloody shirt theme:

> Every unregenerate rebel . . . every deserter, every sneak who ran away from the draft calls himself a Democrat. . . . Every man who labored for the rebellion in the field, who murdered Union prisoners by cruelty and starvation . . . calls himself a Democrat. Every wolf in sheep's clothing who pretends to preach the gospel but proclaims the righteousness of man-selling and slavery; every one who shoots down negroes in the streets, burns up negro school-houses and meeting-houses, and murders women and children by the light of their own flaming dwellings, calls himself a Democrat. . . . In short, the Democratic party may be described as a common sewer and loathsome receptacle, into which is emptied every element of treason North and South, every element of inhumanity and barbarism which has dishonored the age.

The outcome of this raucous campaign was an overwhelming victory for the anti-Johnson Republicans. The proportions of the Republican victory were quite astonishing: they won control of every northern state legislature, won every northern gubernatorial contest, and gained more than two-thirds majorities in both houses of Congress.

Various explanations have been suggested for this result: that the Republicans deceived and misled the voters (though hardly more than the Johnsonians); that northern businessmen gave the Republicans a large campaign fund; and that the veterans, now organized in the Grand Army of the Republic, were mobilized behind the Republicans. All of this was true; but more important was the genuine fear that President Johnson, through his southern governments, was going to lose the peace—that unrepentant rebels were regaining control of the South and re-establishing slavery. When this appeared to be the likely outcome of Johnson's plan of reconstruction, northern voters turned to the Republicans and gave them a mandate to try a reconstruction plan of their own.

CHAPTER FIVE

Radical Reconstruction

After their victory over Johnson, the congressional radicals were suddenly forced to play a role they had never played before: that of responsible men exercising substantial power. Prior to 1866, though having considerable influence, they had always been a minority, and they now found the transition from uninhibited critics to makers of policy far from an easy one. When the radicals and their moderate allies decided to liquidate the Johnson governments in the southern states and to make an entirely new beginning, they had reached the point where they could no longer deal with reconstruction in vague and broad generalities. The time had come for specific legislative enactments and, equally important, for careful assessment of the obstacles they would encounter in striving to achieve their goals. Since the obstacles were sometimes greater than they had anticipated, their enactments were not always successful and occasionally led to unexpected results.

President Johnson, in spite of his defeat, continued to be a formidable problem. Though his vetoes of congressional legislation could be easily overridden, he alone could enforce the laws after they were passed; and in doing so he might give them the narrowest possible interpretation and exploit every defect. A second problem involved the moderate Republicans who presumably had been converted to radicalism. It still remained to be seen how complete and how durable the conversion would be. A third problem was the preservation of unity among the radicals now that the victory had been won; for radicals showed a disturbing tendency toward fragmentation and self-destruction. A final problem was the continued prestige of the old, experienced ruling class of the South, whose success in winning control of the Johnson governments demonstrated its enduring economic and political power. To offset its power the radicals relied upon the four million southern Negroes to create a new political force. Without effective Negro support, their program was bound to fail.

Since the Negroes were crucial figures in radical reconstruction, it is essential to understand their condition at the time they gained their freedom. Most of them had by then lost all but a tiny fragment of their African culture. Though in slavery they had been denied full participation in the white man's culture, their ambition was to become an integral part of American society. They knew how to make a living as freemen, because they had experience as farmers, as skilled craftsmen, as domestic servants, or as unskilled urban laborers. What they still needed were economic opportunities, training in the management of their own affairs, and incentives for diligent toil.

Because the ante-bellum slave codes had prohibited teaching slaves to read or write, only a small minority of Negroes were literate. In this respect, as in most others, slavery had been a poor training school for the responsibilities of citizenship. It gave Negroes few opportunities to develop initiative or to think independently; it discouraged self-reliance; it put a premium on docility and subservience; it indoctrinated Negroes with a sense of their own inferiority; and it instilled in many of them a fear of white men that they would only slowly overcome. A writer in *Harper's Weekly* reminded friends of the Negroes that the freedmen were but "the slaves of yesterday . . . with all the shiftless habits of slavery [to be] unlearned. . . . They come broken in spirit, and with the long, long habit of servility."

Yet there is little evidence that slavery had developed in many of its victims a fondness for bondage. Masters liked to think that their slaves were contented with their lot—and no doubt some of them found it not too painful to adapt to their condition. But the behavior of the slaves during the Civil War removed any doubt about whether the majority of them understood the meaning of freedom and were eager to enjoy its benefits. For as the federal armies advanced, the slaves fled from the plantations by the thousands, and the southern labor system collapsed. A Georgia planter spoke for many others when he complained bitterly about what he regarded as the "ingratitude evinced in the African character." "This war," he wrote, "has taught us the perfect impossibility of placing the least confidence in any Negro. In too numerous instances those we esteemed the most have been the first to desert us. . . . House servants . . . are often the first to have their minds polluted with evil thoughts."

In short, most Negroes, to the dismay of their former masters, joyfully accepted their freedom; and for a time many of them took special pleasure in making use of one of its chief prerogatives: the right to move from place to place without the consent of any white man. An agent of the Freedmen's Bureau gave several reasons for the restlessness of the Negroes immediately after emancipation: they wanted to see new things; they looked for relatives from whom they had been separated in slavery days; they went to the cities in search of work or to find schools for their children. "The shackles suddenly falling off," explained Carl Schurz, "it is by no means wonderful that their first impulse should be to have a holiday. Some felt inclined to use their freedom first in walking a little away from their plantations." Indeed, it was going to take a while for the Negroes to learn how to live as free men. As the *Nation* observed, "No great social revolution ever took place without causing great temporary loss and inconvenience." There was, after all, only one way that the Negroes could learn to live as free men, and that was for them to *start* living as free men—to make mistakes and profit from them.

This was precisely what the radicals proposed that the Negroes should do. The radicals, to reconstruct the South on a firm foundation, would throw out the Black Codes, which were hardly designed to prepare the Negroes for freedom anyway, give the Negroes civil rights and the ballot, and get white men accustomed to treating Negroes as equals, at least politically and legally. Aid to the freedmen was thus at the very heart of radical reconstruction; it was this aspect of the program, and little else, that justified designating as radicals the Republican leaders in Congress. Their attempt to give full citizenship to southern Negroes—in effect, to revolutionize the relations of the two races—was the great "leap in the dark" of the reconstruction era.

Some of the radicals believed that it would be essential to give the Negroes not only civil and political rights but some initial economic assistance as well. These four million people had emerged from bondage in complete destitution, without land, without shelter, without a legal claim even to the clothes on their backs. Neither Lincoln's

V: *Radical Reconstruction*

Emancipation Proclamation nor the Thirteenth Amendment had required masters to make any settlement with their former slaves for past services, or provided for economic aid from the public treasury. In the words of Frederick Douglass, the freedmen "were sent away empty handed, without money, without friends, and without a foot of land to stand upon. Old and young, sick and well, they were turned loose to the open sky, naked to their enemies."

This condition of economic helplessness, some radicals thought, was what threatened to make Negro freedom purely nominal; it was this that enabled the white landholders, with the aid of the Black Codes, to re-establish bondage in another form. The congressional Committee on Reconstruction heard a great deal of convincing testimony about the use of southern vagrancy laws and various extra-legal coercive devices to force Negroes back into agricultural labor under strict discipline. This testimony suggested that there was a close relationship between the securing of civil and political rights on the one hand and the establishment of economic independence on the other.

Near the end of the war, Edwin M. Stanton, Lincoln's Secretary of War, and General Sherman had a conference with twenty Negro leaders in Savannah. During the conference the question arose of how the freedmen could best be prepared to stand on their own feet. The reply of the Negroes was: "The way we can best take care of ourselves is to have land, and . . . till it by our own labor." They were doubtless right, for in the agricultural society of the South white landholders had become so accustomed to exploiting Negro labor that nothing less than a sweeping program of land reform could have changed things very much. Land reform might have been accomplished by assisting the Negroes to take advantage of the Homestead

Act as it was applied to the public lands of the South after the war; or by federal land purchases and resale to Negroes on long-term credits; or by the seizure of land from the former slaveholders.

Though all of these methods were considered, most of the drive for land reform centered on the third alternative, that is, confiscation. Those who favored confiscation justified it, first, as a penalty for treason and, second, as fair compensation to the Negroes for their many years of unrequited toil. This matter of land redistribution, whether achieved through confiscation or in some other way, was one of the most momentous questions the Republicans had to decide. They made their decision before the end of 1867, and it proved to be a crucial one in the development of their program.

The advocates of confiscation hoped to make use of the congressional act of 1862 which had subjected the property of those supporting the rebellion to seizure. But Lincoln, it should be remembered, had forced Congress to limit the time of the forfeitures to the lives of the guilty parties and to permit the return of confiscated lands to their heirs; moreover, he had made no serious attempt to enforce the act. In June 1866 the Johnson administration, holding that the act had been strictly a war measure, ended confiscations. However, the radicals who favored land reform refused to accept this ruling. Indeed, ever since 1862 they had been trying to strengthen the measure, especially to adopt an amendment preventing heirs from recovering forfeited lands.

In 1864, the American Freedmen's Inquiry Commission,[1] appointed by Secretary of War Stanton to visit the South, examine the condition of the Negroes, and make

---

[1] The commission consisted of three members: Robert Dale Owen, Samuel G. Howe, and James McKaye.

policy recommendations, concluded that without land reform a system of serfdom would develop. In the words of one of its members, "No such thing as a free, democratic society can exist in any country where all lands are owned by one class of men and cultivated by another." The commission recommended that the Negroes be made "owners in fee of the farms or gardens they occupy."

Early in 1865, General Sherman, faced with the problem of destitution among the masses of Negroes who had escaped from the plantations, took the first step toward a wholesale redistribution of land in one area of the Deep South. By his Special Field Order Number 15, he set aside the South Carolina and Georgia sea islands south of Charleston and the abandoned rice lands along the rivers for a distance of thirty miles inland for the settlement of Negroes. These lands were to be divided into farms of not more than forty acres, and Negro families were to be given "possessory titles" to them until Congress should decide upon their final disposition. General Rufus Saxton, a friend of the radicals with a genuine concern for the welfare of the freedmen, was appointed Inspector of Settlements and Plantations and placed in charge of the program. Saxton colonized some 40,000 Negroes on the lands under his control, and he presented evidence to the congressional Committee on Reconstruction that the program was a success. But President Johnson saw to it that most of these lands were returned to their original owners, and in January 1866 he removed Saxton.

A smaller but equally promising relocation experiment occurred in Mississippi at a place called Davis Bend, about twenty-five miles south of Vicksburg. Late in the war government officials seized a large tract of land embracing six plantations, including those owned by Jefferson Davis and his brother. Here, in 1864, about seventy-five Negro farmers raised crops which enabled them to make profits ranging as high as $1,000 after repaying credits advanced by the government. The next year, most of this land was divided among some 1,800 Negroes of all ages who organized themselves into companies and partnerships of various kinds. After raising and marketing their crops and paying all expenses, they finished the year with a cash balance on hand of $159,200. Vernon L. Wharton believes that this experiment suggests one of the tragic "might-have-beens" of American history. "A wiser and more benevolent government," he writes, "might well have seen in Davis Bend the suggestion of a long-time program for making the Negro a self-reliant, prosperous, and enterprising element of the population. . . . [Such a program] would certainly have greatly altered the future of the South, and it might have made her a much happier and more prosperous section."[2] Instead, President Johnson pardoned the owners of the Davis Bend plantations, and the land was returned to them.

The debate over land redistribution was resumed when Congress met in December 1865 and continued until early 1867 when that body finally passed a series of reconstruction measures. Sumner insisted that confiscation was a logical part of emancipation; the plantations, he said, "so many nurseries of the Rebellion, must be broken up and the freedmen must have the pieces." Stevens, the strongest advocate of confiscation, reminded his colleagues that "when that wise man the Emperor of Russia set free twenty-two million serfs, he compelled their masters to give them homesteads upon the very soil which they had tilled; . . . 'for,' said he, in noble words, 'they have earned this, they have worked upon the land for ages, and they

---

[2] Vernon Lane Wharton: *The Negro in Mississippi, 1865–1890* (Chapel Hill, 1947), pp. 38–41.

are entitled to it.' " Stevens wondered whether America would do less for its emancipated slaves. "The whole fabric of southern society *must* be changed," he said, "and never can it be done if this opportunity is lost. How can republican institutions, free schools, free churches, free social intercourse exist in a mingled community of nabobs and serfs? . . . If the South is ever to be made a safe Republic let her lands be cultivated by the toil of the owners, or the free labor of intelligent citizens. This must be done even though it drive her nobility into exile."

In elaborating his confiscation plan, Stevens proposed to apply it to about 70,000 of the "chief rebels" who owned some 394,000,000 acres of land. Thus confiscation would affect less than five per cent of the South's white families. He would dispose of the land in this manner: give forty acres to every adult freedman and sell the rest to help pay the public debt, provide pensions for disabled veterans, and compensate loyal men for damage to property suffered during the war. To the objection that it would be inhuman to treat 70,000 southern landlords in this fashion, Stevens recalled Lincoln's proposal to remove the Negroes from the country. "Far easier and more beneficial," he concluded, "to exile 70,000 proud, bloated, and defiant rebels than to expatriate 4,000,000 laborers, native to the soil and loyal to the government."

Another radical who favored confiscation was Representative George W. Julian of Indiana. Julian advocated confiscation because of a long and bitter opposition to monopolies of all kinds, including land monopolies. For the same reason he had opposed the granting of millions of acres of land from the public domain as subsidies to the railroads. In the South he hoped to create a society of independent landowning yeoman farmers, which brought him close to President Johnson as far as economic policy was concerned. The chief difference between them was that Julian desired to include Negroes in his program, for he denied their inferiority and demanded that they be given equal opportunities. To Julian the twin evils of the Old South had been slavery and the land monopoly of the planter class. Confiscation would destroy this monopoly, and the land could then be turned over to Negroes, poor whites, Union veterans, and immigrants. It must not be permitted to fall into the hands of northern capitalists, for Julian believed that this would simply create a new class of land monopolists whose dominion over the freedmen would be "more galling than slavery itself."

The congressional radicals won limited popular support for a program of confiscation. "Given two things," predicted the New York *Independent*, "the negro question solves itself—the easiest of all difficult problems: Land and the Ballot—land, that he may support his family; the ballot, that he may support the state. Grant these to the negro, and . . . he will trouble the nation no more." In defense of Stevens, *Harper's Weekly* declared that "every reflecting man" knew that without land the Negroes lacked "a vital element of substantial citizenship." However, judging from Stevens's mail, the most popular argument in favor of confiscation was that the proceeds from land sales could be used to reduce the public debt and thus to reduce taxes. Once convince the North "that all our taxes are to be removed," wrote A. G. Bemon, "and there will be but one solid vote for the [Republican] party."

But in the end, in spite of arguments such as these, the program of land reform was defeated. The moderate Republicans would not accept it, nor would some Congressmen who were normally counted as radicals. Not even the powers of Sumner and Stevens were great enough to force confiscation into the reconstruction acts of 1867. And this was a severe defeat for radicalism; or at least it defined some rather narrow boundaries within which the radicals could operate. It meant that their program would have only the most limited economic content; that the Negroes' civil and political rights would be in a precarious state for many years to come; and that radical influence in southern politics would probably collapse as soon as federal troops were removed. For the economic degradation of the Negroes strengthened the white man's belief in their innate inferiority, as well as the white man's conviction that for Negroes to possess substantial political power was unnatural, even absurd. The failure of land reform probably made inevitable the ultimate failure of the whole radical program—probably meant that, sooner or later, the southern white landholders and other propertied interests would regain control and re-establish the policies of the Johnson governments.

Why did confiscation—indeed, land reform of any kind —fail to pass Congress? In part it was due to the fact that many of the radicals did not understand the need to give Negro emancipation economic support. Most of them apparently believed that a series of constitutional amendments granting freedom, civil rights, and the ballot would be enough. They seemed to have little conception of what might be called the sociology of freedom, the ease with which mere laws can be flouted when they alone support an economically dependent class, especially a minority group against whom is directed an intense racial prejudice. Even William Lloyd Garrison, the most militant of the old abolitionist leaders, was ready to dissolve the American Anti-Slavery Society after the Thirteenth Amendment had been adopted. To Garrison legal emancipation and civil rights legislation were the primary goals, and the economic plight of the Negroes concerned him a good deal less.

Moreover, confiscation, or even the purchase of land for

the Negroes, would have violated what most Republicans, radical or moderate, regarded as sound economic morality. Government paternalism of this sort would have a blighting influence on the initiative of those who received it. Since the Negro was free, his economic status must be determined by his own enterprise. "Now, we totally deny the assumption that the distribution of other people's land to the negroes is necessary to complete the work of emancipation," declared the *Nation*. Whether the ownership of land will prove a blessing or a curse depends on how the holder has acquired it. "If he has inherited it from an honest father, as most of our farmers have, or has bought it with the proceeds of honest industry, it is pretty sure to prove a blessing. If he has got it by gambling, swindling, or plunder it will prove a curse. . . . A large fortune acquired by cheating, gambling, or robbery is almost sure . . . to kill the soul of him who makes it—to render all labor irksome to him, all gains slowly acquired seem not worth having, and patience and scrupulousness seem marks of imbecility."

In addition, confiscation was an obvious attack on property rights—so much so that it is really more surprising that some of these middle-class radicals favored it, even when applied only to rebels, than that most did not. "A division of rich men's lands amongst the landless . . . would give a shock to our whole social and political system from which it would hardly recover without the loss of liberty," warned the *Nation*. A proposal "in which provision is made for the violation of a greater number of the principles of good government and for the opening of a deeper sink of corruption has never been submitted to a legislative body."

Finally, many business friends of the Republicans saw the propertyless Negroes as a labor reservoir for northern industry, or for southern industry or agriculture in which they might invest. Without exception, Northerners who had purchased southern cotton lands were opposed to confiscation. As a result, the land reformers were outnumbered even in the ranks of the radicals. John Binny told Stevens that the northern states "in monster public meetings would lift their voice in thunder against it. . . . You would lose your majority in Congress."

The Republicans did, however, make one less ambitious attempt to give the freedman federal assistance. The disruption of the plantation system, caused by the war and the abolition of slavery, created such widespread destitution among the Negroes that private benevolence was unable to cope with it. In March 1865 Congress created, as an agency of the War Department, the Bureau of Refugees, Freedmen, and Abandoned Lands, commonly known as the Freedmen's Bureau. It was to provide food, clothing, and medical care for both white refugees and Negro freedmen; to settle them on abandoned or confiscated lands; and in general to help the freedmen in the period of transition from slavery to freedom—to get them back to work, to aid them in their dealings with the landholders, and to provide them with schools. But according to the original act, the bureau's work was to terminate within a year after the end of the war.

The congressional Committee on Reconstruction, however, collected much evidence indicating that the bureau needed not only to have its life extended but to be given additional power. The committee found that landholders were using the Black Codes to take advantage of the Negroes and were combining to keep down the wages of agricultural labor. Sometimes they bound Negroes to unfair labor contracts; sometimes they refused to pay them wages at all. The committee also found that Negroes were not always receiving fair trials in state and local courts, and that they were often maltreated by individual whites or by organized bands of "regulators." Therefore Congress, in February 1866, passed a new Freedmen's Bureau bill indefinitely extending the agency's life, increasing its power to supervise labor contracts, and authorizing it to establish special courts for Negroes when they were unable to get justice in the regular courts. In his veto message President Johnson argued that the bill was unnecessary and an unconstitutional violation of the rights of the states; but Congress eventually overrode the President's veto.

The bureau, though competently and conscientiously directed by General Oliver O. Howard, was highly unpopular with most white Southerners and has since been subjected to severe criticism. Its critics accused it of meddling in matters that were not properly within the jurisdiction of the federal government; of stirring up discontent among the Negroes and filling them with false hopes; of employing corrupt or incompetent administrators who wasted federal money; and of acting as a political agency for the Republican party. There was some truth in several of these charges. Some of the bureau agents did tell the Negroes that they were going to get land, not for the purpose of deceiving them but because the agents believed, or hoped, that Congress would actually give them land. Some of the agents were incompetent, some were corrupt, and some used the bureau's power to win Negro votes for the Republicans.

Such criticism, however, does not comprise a full appraisal of the bureau's work. Those who objected to it on the ground that the plight of the southern Negro was no concern of the federal government were, in effect, objecting to assistance of any kind; for Negro destitution was clearly a national problem which the individual southern states had neither the resources nor the desire to deal with.

V: *Radical Reconstruction*

Actually, the most valid criticism that can be made of the Republican majority in Congress in this respect is that it failed to give the bureau sufficient power and funds to perform efficiently its manifold duties. As for the complaint that bureau agents stirred up discontent among the Negroes, the basis for it in most cases was that they encouraged Negroes to demand land, civil rights, and political enfranchisement. No doubt some agents did incite the freedmen in this fashion, and no doubt they distressed those who preferred to regulate race relations with some form of Black Code. White men who were accustomed to the humble, subservient Negro of slavery days were bound to find any change in his character unpleasant, any claim to equality almost intolerable. Insofar as the Freedmen's Bureau contributed to this result, it played a constructive role in the transformation of the Negro from slave to citizen.

There was, in fact, cause for criticizing numerous agents of the bureau for quite the opposite reason, that is, for showing no sympathy for, or interest in, the Negroes. Some agents allied themselves with the southern landowners and adopted their view that Negroes are by nature lazier and more shiftless than white men and need greater compulsion to make them work. Vernon L. Wharton's study of bureau activities in Mississippi shows that some agents co-operated with the planters to coerce Negroes, directly or indirectly, to remain on the land. One agent even whipped Negroes for their white employers when they were recalcitrant. In these and other cases, agents simply fell under the control of the white landholders among whom they lived and whose good opinion they sought to win. But in spite of cases such as these, the southern tradition holds that bureau agents were united in a determination to make life miserable for white men.

The tradition that the bureau was rife with corruption

and incompetence is also an exaggeration. In 1866, President Johnson, seeking ammunition to use against the radicals, appointed a commission, consisting of General Joseph S. Fullerton and General James B. Steedman, to make a thorough investigation of the bureau's activities. The commission was as hostile to the bureau as Johnson himself. In North Carolina it uncovered a major scandal, but a scandal of little use to Johnson, for it involved the cheating and mistreating of Negroes, not whites. Elsewhere the commission turned up so little that would help the President that its tour of the southern states was cut short and finally abandoned. In the words of a recent scholar: "President Johnson . . . had gained from the Steedman-Fullerton investigation . . . little but laughter from the Radicals. . . . His best efforts to discredit the Freedman's Bureau had failed."[3]

A balanced evaluation of the Freedmen's Bureau, therefore, must stress its constructive achievements. First, while trying to make the Negroes self-supporting as soon as possible, the bureau provided emergency relief for those who were in desperate need. During its brief existence it issued more than fifteen million rations and gave medical care to a million people. Second, it spent more than $5,000,000 for Negro schools, a pitifully inadequate sum but as much as Congress would grant. Usually the bureau furnished buildings and other physical facilities, while private benevolent societies provided teachers and books; together they established the first schools for Negroes in the southern states. Third, the bureau tried to prevent landowners from taking advantage of the Negroes. It set aside some of the provisions of the Black Codes, saw to it that Negroes were free to choose their employers, fixed the

---

[3] George R. Bentley: *A History of the Freedmen's Bureau* (Philadelphia, 1955), p. 133.

conditions of labor, and supervised the making and enforcement of labor contracts. Finally, the bureau tried to protect the Negroes' civil rights. Because of the legal discriminations of the Johnson governments, local administrators either established special freedmen's courts to handle their cases or sent observers into the regular courts to make sure that trials were conducted fairly. Though a system of special courts for Negroes was obviously undesirable as a permanent arrangement, there seemed at the time to be no other way in some localities to avoid flagrant injustice.

But in 1869, with its work scarcely begun, Congress provided for the termination of the bureau's activities, and soon after it ceased to exist. Even a Congress dominated by the radical-moderate coalition could support an experiment in social engineering for only a few short years, and it had to be justified on the grounds of an unprecedented emergency. Thus ended the one modest federal effort to deal directly with some of the social and economic problems confronting the postwar South.

The liquidation of the Freedmen's Bureau also meant that Congress had lost its most efficient agency to protect Negroes in the enjoyment of the civil and political rights they had recently been given. Congress had provided federal guarantees of civil rights to all persons, first by the Civil Rights Act passed over Johnson's veto in 1866, then by the Fourteenth Amendment ratified by the states in 1868. The Civil Rights Act clearly conferred citizenship on American Negroes: it declared that "all persons born in the United States and not subject to any foreign power, excluding Indians not taxed," are citizens of the United States. This act removed the doubts about the Negroes' status which had been raised before the war when the Supreme Court, in the Dred Scott case, held that Negroes

were not citizens, and when the State Department sometimes refused to give Negroes passports. In addition, the
Civil Rights Act provided that citizens "of every race and
color" were to have equal rights in all states to make contracts, to sue, to testify in court, to purchase, hold, and dispose of real and personal property, and were to enjoy "full
and equal benefit of all laws and proceedings for the security of person and property." Finally, all citizens were
to be subjected "to like punishment, pains and penalties,
and to none other." Violations of this law carried penalties of fine and imprisonment, and the Executive Department and federal courts were given ample powers to
enforce it.

Fearing that the Supreme Court might rule against the
constitutionality of the Civil Rights Act, the Joint
Committee on Reconstruction, after much wrangling, incorporated its substance into the first section of the Fourteenth Amendment. This section, as revised in the Senate,
was a compromise between radical and moderate Republicans—few were entirely satisfied with it, but all of them
eventually gave it their support. First, it defined American
citizenship: "All persons born or naturalized in the
United States, and subject to the jurisdiction thereof, are
citizens of the United States and of the State wherein they
reside." Then, in terms that were both broad and vague,
it prohibited the states from enacting laws "which shall
abridge the privileges or immunities of citizens of the
United States"; from depriving "any person of life, liberty, or property, without due process of law"; and (most
important in recent years) from denying "to any person
within its jurisdiction the equal protection of the laws."

For many years after reconstruction, as we know, the
Fourteenth Amendment was almost a dead letter as far as
the civil rights of Negroes were concerned; but the federal

courts enforced it vigorously when any state tried to regulate railroads or other corporations. In law, corporations are "persons," and the courts repeatedly invalidated regulatory legislation as violations of the "due process" clause of this amendment. With this in mind, historians who stressed an economic interpretation of radical reconstruction insisted that the real, though secret, motive of the authors of the amendment was to protect corporations rather than Negroes. They based their case on the testimony of two members of the Joint Committee on Reconstruction who helped to frame the amendment. Representative John A. Bingham, who wrote the "due process" clause, claimed several years later that he had phrased it "word for word and syllable for syllable" to protect the rights of property. Still later, in 1882, Roscoe Conkling of New York, who was then representing a railroad corporation before the Supreme Court, declared: "At the time the Fourteenth Amendment was ratified, individuals and joint stock companies were appealing for congressional and administrative protection against invidious and discriminating state and local taxes. . . . Those who devised the Fourteenth Amendment wrote in grave sincerity. They planted in the Constitution a monumental truth. . . . That truth is but the Golden Rule, so entrenched as to curb the many who would do to the few as they would not have the few do to them."

Of course, we cannot read the minds of those who framed the Fourteenth Amendment, but there is no contemporary evidence—nothing in the records of the Joint Committee or in the congressional debates—to indicate any thought at the time of giving protection to private corporations. Bingham's and Conkling's ex post facto arguments provide rather weak evidence; hence the case for an economic interpretation of Republican motivation must be regarded as unproved. There is, in fact, no reason to reject the explanation that Thad Stevens gave when the amendment was being discussed in Congress. Its purpose, he said, was "to correct the unjust legislation of the states [that is, the Black Codes], so . . . that the law which operates upon one man shall operate *equally* upon all. . . . Whatever law punishes a white man . . . shall punish the black man precisely in the same way and to the same degree. . . . Whatever law allows the white man to testify in court shall allow the man of color to do the same."

A far more significant question is how the framers of the Fourteenth Amendment defined civil rights and precisely which ones they intended to protect—a question that pro- and anti-segregationists are still debating today. It is reasonably clear that they intended to prohibit the states from governing Negroes by special Black Codes, from making certain acts felonies for Negroes but not for whites, from providing more severe penalties for Negro felons than for white, and from excluding Negro testimony in cases involving whites. It is doubtful, however, that most of them regarded the exclusion of Negroes from jury service, or anti-miscegenation laws, or the segregation of Negroes in public places as violations of civil rights. Few of the moderates would have thought so, and apparently not even all of the radicals did.

Actually, neither the radicals nor the Negroes of the reconstruction era considered social segregation to be the most urgent immediate issue. Though resenting it and occasionally speaking out against it, most Negro leaders acquiesced in segregation for the time being, in order to concentrate upon obtaining security of person, equality in the courts, and political rights. In the South the informal pattern of social segregation established for free Negroes in prewar years and enforced under the Johnson governments was challenged only sporadically. Nearly all of the schools subsidized by the Freedmen's Bureau were racially segregated. When Congress, in 1866, appropriated money for the schools of the District of Columbia, it again either approved of, or acquiesced in, a system of segregation. In fact, Senator Henry Wilson, a radical, admitted that a special system of Negro schools had been established and explained that the appropriation bill simply provided that "those in the colored schools will receive the same benefit that those receive who are in the white schools"—a fairly clear statement of the doctrine of "separate but equal." In short, most of the Congressmen who voted for the Fourteenth Amendment, and the states that ratified it, probably did not intend to outlaw state-enforced racial segregation. But the terms of the amendment, as we have seen, are broad and vague; and when the Supreme Court outgrew the sociology of the nineteenth century, it began to discover new meaning in the loose phrase "equal protection of the laws."

At least a few of the radicals, notably Senator Charles Sumner, believed from the start that they were proscribing segregation. Beginning with the reconstruction acts of 1867, Sumner tried, unsuccessfully, to require the southern states to establish "public schools open to all without distinction of race or color." For the next seven years, until his death in 1874, he urged his colleagues to subsidize biracial public schools, to desegregate the schools of the District of Columbia, and, above all, to adopt a Civil Rights Act that would outlaw all forms of racial segregation as violations of the Fourteenth Amendment. The debate on Sumner's numerous bills ran the gamut of arguments that have been heard ever since. The segregationists, North and South, denied that a separation of the races was a violation of civil rights, or that the Fourteenth

Amendment was designed to interfere with matters that are purely social; and they warned that an attempt to integrate the public schools would simply destroy the system altogether. Sumner replied that segregated schools were "an ill disguised violation of the principle of equality," and that they injured the personalities of white children as well as Negro. "Pharisaism of race," he said, "becomes an element of character, when, like all other Pharisaisms it should be stamped out."

Sumner did not live to see a Civil Rights Act adopted, but the year after his death his long labors bore some fruit. In 1875, Congress passed an act whose preamble declared: "[It] is essential to just government [that] we recognize the equality of all men before the law, and . . . it is the duty of government in its dealings with the people to mete out equal and exact justice to all, of whatever nativity, race, color, or persuasion, religious or political." The act itself guaranteed to all persons, regardless of race or color, "the full and equal enjoyment of the accommodations . . . of inns, public conveyances on land or water, theatres, and other places of public amusement." It also prohibited the disqualification of citizens for jury service "on account of race, color, or previous condition of servitude." But there was not a word in the act about public schools—every effort to include them in its terms was defeated.

The Civil Rights Act of 1875 was significant nonetheless, because it was the first federal attempt to deal directly with social segregation and discrimination by the states or by private enterprises established to serve the public. "It is the completion of the promise of equal civil rights," said *Harper's Weekly*. "Honest legislation upon the subject will not at once remove all prejudice, but it will clear the way for its disappearance." In 1883, however, in a group of civil rights cases, the Supreme Court invalidated

140

the act. It endorsed the position of the segregationists that the Fourteenth Amendment had not given Congress jurisdiction over the social relationships of the two races. There matters stood for the next seventy years.[4]

On the question of Negro suffrage, the Republicans eventually took a bolder and less ambiguous stand than they did on the question of segregation, but only after several years of hesitation and evasion. In the autumn of 1865 even Thad Stevens was noncommittal when he spoke to his constituents: "Whether those who have fought our battles should all be allowed to vote, or only those of a paler hue, I leave to be discussed in the future when Congress can take legitimate cognizance of it." But in most cases the radicals' early timidity resulted less from their own doubts than from their fear of public opinion in the North. Radicals were embarrassed by the fact that in most of the northern states the Negroes were then disenfranchised, and that in recent years the voters in several of them had rejected proposals to give Negroes the ballot.

As a result, few radicals made an explicit demand for Negro suffrage during the congressional elections of 1866, and the Fourteenth Amendment got at the matter only by indirection. The second section of the amendment simply provided that when a state denied adult male citizens the right to vote for reasons other than participation in rebellion or other crimes, such state was to have its representation in Congress reduced proportionately—a provision, incidentally, which in subsequent years was totally ignored. This weak and ineffective approach to Negro suffrage—the result of another compromise between radicals and moderates—caused Stevens privately to call the Fourteenth Amendment a "shilly-shally bungling thing," and

---

[4] The court did not invalidate that part of the act which prohibited the exclusion of Negroes from jury service.

Wendell Phillips to call it a "fatal and total surrender." "Of course, no man could afford to vote against the proposition," recalled George W. Julian, but it was "a wanton betrayal of justice and humanity. Congress, however, was unprepared for more thorough work. The conservative policy . . . was obliged, as usual, to feel its way cautiously, and wait on the logic of events; while the negro . . . was finally indebted for the franchise to the desperate madness of his enemies in rejecting the dishonorable proposition of his friends."

After their victory in the elections of 1866, the Republicans were, in the words of one of them, less "smitten by unnatural fear" and more inclined to recognize Negro suffrage as the "grand and all-comprehending" issue. Now they passed an act enfranchising the Negroes in the District of Columbia; and in their reconstruction measures of 1867, they required the southern states to write Negro suffrage into their constitutions. Finally, in 1869, after another relapse into timidity during the presidential election the previous year, the Republicans passed the Fifteenth Amendment, which unequivocally declared: "The right of the citizens of the United States to vote shall not be denied or abridged by the United States or by any State on account of race, color, or previous condition of servitude." The amendment was ratified by 1870; and thus, said the *Nation*, "the agitation against slavery has reached an appropriate and triumphant conclusion."

On reflection, however, the *Nation*, like many others, thought it would have been better to admit the Negroes to the franchise gradually, "and through an educational test." Some had suggested that Negro suffrage be postponed until 1876. Representative Julian presented the ablest defense of the almost immediate enfranchisement of the Negroes even though the great mass of them were illiterate. A literacy test, he argued, is "a singularly insufficient measure of fitness. Reading and writing are mechanical processes, and a man may be able to perform them without any worthiness of life or character. . . . If penmanship must be made the avenue to the ballot, I fear several honorable gentlemen on this floor will be disfranchised." Julian observed that more than a half million illiterate white men were permitted to vote, and no one proposed to take the ballot away from them. He concluded: "By no means would I disparage education, and especially political training; but the ballot is itself a schoolmaster. If you expect a man to use it well you must place it in his hands, and let him learn to cast it by trial. . . . If you wish to teach the ignorant man, black or white, how to vote, you must grant him the *right* to vote as the first step in his education."

When the Republicans turned from the Negroes to the white men of the South who had supported the rebellion, their reconstruction measures were remarkably lenient. The fourth section of the Fourteenth Amendment prohibited the southern states from paying any Confederate debt or any claim for emancipated slave property.[5] This amendment, in its third section, also withheld from the President the power to restore, by presidential pardon, political rights to Confederate leaders. As it was reported by the Joint Committee on Reconstruction, this section would have excluded those who had supported the Confederacy from voting in federal elections until July 4, 1870. "Here is the mildest of all punishments ever inflicted on traitors," said Stevens. "I would be glad to see it extended to 1876, and to include all State and municipal as well as national elections." Instead, the Senate softened it. In its final form it provided that persons who had held state or federal offices before the rebellion, and who had

---

[5] It also provided that the "validity of the public debt of the United States . . . shall not be questioned."

then supported the rebellion, were to be ineligible for public office until pardoned by a two-thirds vote of Congress. This disability applied to virtually the entire political leadership of the ante-bellum South; but for most of them it lasted only until 1872, when Congress passed a sweeping amnesty act. After that, all but a few of them were eligible once more to run for public office.

On March 2, 1867, the Republicans passed an act outlining their general plan of political reconstruction. Three subsequent acts, adopted on March 23 and July 19, 1867, and March 11, 1868, cleared up points left vague in the first act, provided machinery for the program's implementation, and established safeguards against presidential obstructionism. President Johnson, of course, vetoed these measures, but Congress passed them quickly and easily over his vetoes. Thus, two years after the end of the war, the process of reconstruction was begun anew. That Thad Stevens and the radicals now had their way may be attributed, first, to Johnson's recalcitrance to the very end; second, to the refusal of ten southern states to accept the terms of the Fourteenth Amendment; and, third, to the continued mistreatment of southern Negroes and Unionists.

These reconstruction acts were based on the assumption, as stated in the preamble of the first act, that "no legal State governments or adequate protection for life or property now exists in the rebel States." The purpose of the acts was to enforce "peace and good order . . . in said States until loyalty and republican State governments can be legally established." To this end, the Johnson governments were repudiated and the ten unreconstructed southern states divided into five military districts.[6] The district

---

[6] The first district consisted of Virginia; the second of the Carolinas; the third of Georgia, Alabama, and Florida; the fourth of Mississippi and Arkansas; the fifth of Louisiana and Texas.

commanders were given broad powers to "protect all persons in their rights of person and property, to suppress insurrection, disorder, and violence, and to punish . . . all disturbers of the public peace." They could, when necessary, remove civil officeholders, make arrests, try civilians in military courts, and use federal troops to preserve order.

The district commanders were also given the responsibility of putting the new program of political reconstruction in motion. They were to enroll the qualified voters, including Negroes but excluding those barred from holding office by the Fourteenth Amendment, and to hold elections for delegates to state constitutional conventions. Each convention was to frame a new constitution providing for Negro suffrage; and when the constitution was ratified by popular vote, a governor and state legislature could be elected. The first legislature was to ratify the Fourteenth Amendment. Finally, after Congress had approved of the new state constitution and after the Fourteenth Amendment had become part of the federal Constitution, the state would be entitled to representation in Congress. Meanwhile, however, the civil government of the state was to be deemed "provisional only, and in all respects subject to the paramount authority of the United States." When elections were held under such provisional government, those disqualified by the Fourteenth Amendment were not to be entitled to vote.

By 1868, six of the southern states had completed this reconstruction process and were readmitted. Four states—Virginia, Georgia, Mississippi, and Texas—delayed until after the Fourteenth Amendment had been ratified and the Fifteenth Amendment had been adopted by Congress. They were therefore required to ratify the Fifteenth Amendment as well. The Republican terms were then fully defined, and by 1870 political reconstruction had been completed in all of the southern states.

There was, however, another aspect of congressional reconstruction: an attempt to alter the relationship of the legislative and executive branches by placing certain restrictions on the powers of the President.[7] In a dramatic assertion of congressional supremacy, the Republicans took precautions against a possible attempt by Johnson to overthrow their rule by military coup. The friends of the President asserted that the present Congress was an illegal body, because the southern states were not represented in it; and a few daring men urged Johnson to use military force to dissolve Congress and to call new elections. Though the President had no taste for a stroke as bold as this, the Republicans took no chances.

First, on January 22, 1867, Congress arrogated the right to call itself into special session, a power heretofore recognized as belonging exclusively to the President. It provided that the first session of the Fortieth Congress

---

[7] The Supreme Court played a passive role in the years of reconstruction, and its prestige declined considerably. Threatened with various reorganization schemes under consideration in Congress, the Court avoided passing on the constitutionality of any of the reconstruction measures. In *Mississippi* vs. *Johnson* (1867) and *Georgia* vs. *Stanton* (1867), it was asked to enjoin the President and the Secretary of War from enforcing the reconstruction acts on the ground that they were unconstitutional. But in each case the Court evaded the issue and ruled that it had no power to enjoin an executive officer "in the performance of his official duties." Another case, *Ex parte McCardle* (1868), involved a Mississippi editor who had been tried before a military commission for criticizing radical reconstruction. An appeal to the Supreme Court challenged the jurisdiction of the military commission and asked for a writ of habeas corpus; but Congress, on March 27, 1868, passed a law denying it appellate jurisdiction in cases involving the right to a writ of habeas corpus. The Court used this law as an excuse for refusing to hear the McCardle case. Finally, in *Texas* vs. *White* (1869), the Court ruled that the southern ordinances of secession had been null and void and that the southern states had never ceased to be states in the federal Union. Though it thus rejected Sumner's "state suicide" theory and Stevens's "conquered province" theory, the Court again declined to consider the constitutionality of radical reconstruction.

(elected in 1866) was to begin on March 4, 1867, rather than at the normal time the following December. The purpose of the Republicans was to avoid another long interval between sessions, when Johnson would again be free to pursue his own policies.

Next, on March 2, in a "rider" attached to an Army Appropriation Act, Congress restricted Johnson's power as commander in chief of the armed forces. The President and Secretary of War were to issue military orders only through the "General of the Army" (who was Ulysses S. Grant); the headquarters of the General of the Army were to be at Washington; and he was not to be removed or sent elsewhere without the consent of the Senate.

Finally, the Tenure of Office Act, also passed on March 2, 1867, was designed to prevent Johnson from using his patronage power against the Republicans as he had done in the congressional elections of 1866. The act provided that a civil officeholder, appointed with the consent of the Senate, was to serve until a successor had been nominated by the President and approved by the Senate. If the Senate rejected the proposed successor, the incumbent was to remain in office. When the Senate was not in session, the President could suspend an incumbent and make a temporary replacement; but if the Senate did not approve the change at its next meeting, the incumbent would "forthwith resume the functions of his office." The act referred specifically to members of the Cabinet: they were to hold their positions "during the term of the President by whom they may have been appointed, and for one month thereafter, subject to removal by and with the advice and consent of the Senate." The purpose of this provision was to prevent Johnson from removing Secretary of War Stanton, the sole remaining member of the Cabinet who sympathized with the radicals.

Not satisfied with these restrictive laws, some radicals thought that a way ought to be found to remove Johnson from office. They were convinced that he was a traitor, that he would sabotage the congressional program, and that he was conniving to return southern rebels and northern Copperheads to power. There is, however, only one constitutional way to remove a President who does not voluntarily resign, and that is by impeachment for high crimes or misdemeanors. On strictly legal grounds Johnson had done nothing to provide a basis for such proceedings.

Nevertheless, on January 7, 1867, the House adopted a resolution, introduced by Representative James M. Ashley of Ohio, instructing the Judiciary Committee to "inquire into the conduct of Andrew Johnson." The resulting investigation was long and thorough. The Judiciary Committee, aided by the Pinkerton detective agency, considered charges that Johnson had illegally returned property to southern rebels, that he had pardoned men who were still traitors at heart, that he had abused his veto power, and that he was implicated in the plot to assassinate Lincoln. None of these charges stood up under examination, and on June 3, 1867, the committee decided by a vote of 5 to 4 not to recommend impeachment.

Then Johnson's aggressive opposition to congressional reconstruction gave new life to the movement for his removal. First, on June 20, 1867, he issued orders to the commanders of the five southern military districts which curtailed their powers and strengthened the positions of the civil governments he had previously created.[8] Second, in the late summer and autumn of 1867, Johnson removed all district commanders who gave evidence of sympathy

---

[8] It was these orders that necessitated the passage of a third reconstruction act on July 19, 1867.

for the radical program. Third, in his annual message of December 2, 1867, he boldly told Congress that in certain cases he "would be compelled to stand on his rights, and maintain them, regardless of consequences." These threats were enough to reverse the decision of the Judiciary Committee, which now, by a vote of 5 to 4, recommended impeachment. In its report the committee majority accused Johnson of "usurpations of power" and charged that his aim was to reconstruct the southern states "in accordance with his own will, in the interests of the great criminals who carried them into the rebellion." The majority maintained that Johnson's offenses did not have to be of the kind for which he could be legally indicted. In a separate report the minority insisted that evidence must be presented that Johnson had committed an indictable crime or misdemeanor; yet "there is not a particle of evidence before us which would be received by any court in the land." On December 7, 1867, the House, by a vote of 57 to 108, rejected the committee's impeachment resolution.

Soon after this vote the whole situation changed when Johnson, after months of indecision, attempted to dismiss the radical Stanton from his Cabinet. In August 1867, while the Senate was not in session, he had suspended Stanton and persuaded General Grant to accept an ad interim appointment as Secretary of War. Convinced that the Tenure of Office Act was unconstitutional, Johnson hoped to get a test case into the federal courts and believed that he had Grant's promise to co-operate with him to that end. Grant, however, had no taste for such a role; and when the Senate refused to approve of Stanton's removal, Grant immediately withdrew in favor of Stanton. The angry President publicly denounced Grant for his "treachery," thus driving the injured and slightly confused General into an alliance with the radicals. Finally, on February 21, 1868, Johnson appointed General Lorenzo Thomas Secretary of War ad interim and formally notified Stanton of his dismissal. But Stanton, encouraged by the radicals, refused to surrender to the President and barricaded himself in his quarters at the War Department, leaving Thomas with little to do but attend meetings of the Cabinet.

Johnson's attempt to remove Stanton, presumably in violation of the Tenure of Office Act, brought to a peak the sense of outrage that had been growing in Congress and in the North. On February 24, 1868, while in this mood, the House, by a vote of 126 to 47, resolved "That Andrew Johnson, President of the United States, be impeached of high crimes and misdemeanors in office." Having voted to impeach Johnson, the House then provided for the appointment of a committee of seven to prepare articles of impeachment.[9] This was a curious order of procedure: first to decide upon impeachment and then to assemble the evidence that was to justify such action.

On March 2 and 3, 1868, the House adopted eleven articles of impeachment. The first eight articles related in one way or another to Johnson's attempted removal of Stanton, whereby Johnson "did then and there commit and was guilty of a high misdemeanor in office."[1] The ninth article accused him of a rather technical violation of the terms of the Army Appropriation Act of March 2, 1867, "with the further intent . . . to prevent the execution of the [Tenure of Office Act]." The tenth article, though it had no substance from a legal standpoint, was actually the

---

[9] The committee consisted of John A. Bingham (Ohio), George S. Boutwell (Mass.), George W. Julian (Ind.), John A. Logan (Ill.), Thaddeus Stevens (Pa.), Hamilton Ward (N.Y.), and James F. Wilson (Ia.).

[1] A violation of the Tenure of Office Act was, by the terms of the act, a "high misdemeanor" carrying a penalty of fine and imprisonment.

heart of the radicals' case. Johnson, it said, "unmindful of the high duties of his office, and the dignity and proprieties thereof, and of the harmony and courtesies which ought to exist and be maintained between the executive and legislative branches of the government . . . did attempt to bring into disgrace, ridicule, hatred, contempt and reproach the Congress of the United States." The article cited various occasions when Johnson publicly made, "with a loud voice, certain intemperate, inflammatory, and scandalous harangues, and did therein utter loud threats and bitter menaces." These harangues were "peculiarly indecent and unbecoming in the Chief Magistrate of the United States, by means whereof said Andrew Johnson has brought the high office of the President of the United States into contempt, ridicule, and disgrace, to the great scandal of all good citizens." The eleventh article repeated the charges in the previous articles and accused Johnson further of referring to the Thirty-ninth Congress as "a Congress of only a part of the United States," thereby bringing into question the legality of its acts.

On March 5 the trial began before the Senate with Chief Justice Salmon P. Chase presiding. Seven impeachment managers appointed by the House, of whom George S. Boutwell and Benjamin F. Butler of Massachusetts and Thaddeus Stevens were leaders, handled the prosecution.[2] Johnson was defended by four able lawyers, among them Henry Stanbery who resigned as Attorney General to represent him.

The impeachment managers developed two separate and somewhat contradictory arguments. They claimed

---

[2] The four other managers were John A. Bingham (Ohio), John A. Logan (Ill.), Thomas Williams (Pa.), and James F. Wilson (Ia.). During the trial Stevens became so ill and feeble that he had to be carried to and from the sessions in a chair. For this reason Butler became the chief of the impeachment managers.

that Johnson, by his attempt to remove Stanton and by his attacks on Congress, was in fact guilty of high crimes and misdemeanors within the meaning of the Constitution. But they also claimed that impeachment was a political rather than a judicial procedure—that the Senate was not a court and therefore needed only to decide whether Johnson was "longer fit to retain the office of President," not whether he had committed an indictable offense. This latter argument was important, first, because it suggested that the radicals were not sure of their case on strict legal grounds, and, second, because they were consequently trying to transform the process of impeachment into a political weapon against the President. Many Republicans took the position, as the *Nation* explained, that impeachment "is an allowable means of getting rid of an executive officer whose administration the majority believe to be injurious to the public welfare."

Insofar as the trial involved legal and constitutional issues, the defense had by far the better case. When Johnson's lawyers argued that impeachment was a judicial process and that the Senate was acting as a court, the law and all the precedents were on their side. If impeachment were made a mere political device, they warned, the constitutional system of checks and balances would be destroyed. Moreover, it was not a crime to try to test the constitutionality of the Tenure of Office Act in the courts. Then the final blow: this act provided that Cabinet officers were to serve during the term of the President who appointed them and for one month thereafter. But Lincoln had appointed Stanton, not Johnson, and the attempt to remove Stanton was therefore not even a technical violation of the act!

On May 16, 1868, the Senate voted on the eleventh article of impeachment, which was the broadest in scope. The vote was 35 for conviction to 19 against—one vote short of the two-thirds majority required to find Johnson guilty as charged. On May 26, after a strenuous effort to persuade one of the dissenters to change his vote, the Senate voted on the second and third articles, but the outcome was exactly the same as on the first vote. With that the radicals gave up, and the Senate adjourned without bothering to vote on the remaining articles of impeachment. The minority that had saved Johnson consisted of twelve Democrats and seven Republicans. For a time the Republican dissenters had to endure bitter criticism, but public opinion swung around to their point of view with surprising speed.[3] In retrospect, Senator John Sherman, who had voted for conviction reluctantly, declared that he was "entirely satisfied with the result."

The radicals' attempt to remove Johnson may be explained in part by the passions of the hour, in part by Johnson's extremely provocative behavior. Had they succeeded in making impeachment a political process, they might have weakened somewhat the independence of the President and the constitutional system of checks and balances. Senator Lyman Trumbull, one of the dissenting Republicans, declared: "Once set the example of impeaching a President for what, when the excitement of the hour shall have subsided, will be regarded as insufficient cause, and no future President will be safe who happens to differ with a majority of the House and two-thirds of the Senate on any measure deemed by them important." Trumbull may have been right, but in estimating the dimensions of this threat, it should be remembered that no President since Johnson has had two thirds of the Senate against

---

[3] The seven dissenting Republicans were William P. Fessenden (Me.), Joseph S. Fowler (Tenn.), James W. Grimes (Ia.), John B. Henderson (Mo.), Edmund G. Ross (Kan.), Lyman Trumbull (Ill.), and Peter G. Van Winkle (W. Va.).

him. Johnson's removal would more likely have been a curiosity of American political history than a precedent for future action.

In behalf of the radicals it may at least be said that they were dealing with a very difficult problem in American politics—one that has plagued the country on several critical occasions. This problem occurs whenever the President and Congress are hostile toward one another and work at cross purposes. For this there is only one legal remedy, and that is for the President to resign voluntarily. Since Johnson, like all other American Presidents, rejected this remedy, the radicals sought another solution. The argument in the tenth article of the impeachment charges, that "harmony . . . ought to exist and be maintained between the executive and legislative branches," was the most telling point in the radical case.

But Johnson was acquitted and was thus able to finish the last few months of his administration.[4] On March 4, 1869, when his term expired, he went home to East Tennessee; but in 1874, after the conservatives regained control of his state, he was elected once more to the United States Senate. Johnson made his last speech in that body on March 22, 1875. It was another blistering attack on radical reconstruction, and his last words were "God save the Constitution." A few months later he suffered a paralytic stroke, and on July 31 he died. He was buried with a copy of the Constitution.

---

[4] Stanton resigned as Secretary of War as soon as the trial ended and was replaced by General John M. Schofield.

CHAPTER SIX

Radical Rule in the South

When Lord Bryce, in the 1880's, wrote *The American Commonwealth*, he commented at length on the southern state governments created under the radical plan of reconstruction. What he had to say about them was not remarkable for its originality, but a few passages are worth quoting to give the flavor of the approaching historical consensus. "Such a Saturnalia of robbery and jobbery has seldom been seen in any civilized country. . . . The position of these [radical] adventurers was like that of a Roman provincial governor in the latter days of the Republic. . . . [All] voting power lay with those who were wholly unfit for citizenship, and had no interest as taxpayers, in good government. . . . [Since] the legislatures were reckless and corrupt, the judges for the most part subservient, the Federal military officers bound to support what purported to be the constitutional authorities of the State, Congress distant and little inclined to listen to the complaints of those whom it distrusted as rebels, greed was unchecked and roguery unabashed."[1] In drawing this unpleasant picture Lord Bryce anticipated the generalizations of the Dunningites, as did many others.

---

[1] James Bryce: *The American Commonwealth*, 3 vols. (New York, 1888), Vol. II, pp. 476–8.

Each of the eleven states of the former Confederacy, during all or part of the decade between 1867 and 1877, fell under the control of the radical Republicans. Tennessee was the first to be captured by them—indeed, it never had a Johnson government—but it was also the first to be lost. Tennessee was "redeemed," as southern white Democrats liked to call their return to power, as early as 1869. The last three states to be redeemed were South Carolina, Florida, and Louisiana, where the radical regimes lasted until the spring of 1877.

What, according to the conservatives, were the sins of the radical governments? The new governments, they said, expelled from power the South's experienced statemen and natural leaders and replaced them with untrained men who were almost uniformly incompetent and corrupt. Among the radical leaders, the Yankee carpetbaggers, crafty adventurers who invaded the postwar South for political and economic plunder, were the most notorious. The scalawags, who assisted the carpetbaggers, were mostly degraded and depraved poor whites, betrayers of their race and section who sought a share of the radical spoils. The Negroes, ignorant and illiterate, played an essentially passive political role, casting their votes as radical agents of the Union League and Freedmen's Bureau told them to. Since the members of the radical coalition owned little or no property themselves, they increased state and local taxes until they came near to ruining the whole class of white property holders. Their extravagant appropriations, their waste, fraud, and corruption, caused shocking increases in southern state debts and brought some states to the edge of bankruptcy. Finally, said the conservatives, the radical governments threatened to destroy the white civilization of the South and to reduce it to African barbarism.

We must first consider the charge that the radicals expelled from power the South's natural leaders. One of the characters in Margaret Mitchell's popular novel, *Gone With the Wind*, complains that everybody who was anybody in the good old days was nobody in the radical regimes. A conservative Tennesseean reported that the radicals in his state were "the party paying no taxes, riding poor horses, wearing dirty shirts, and having no use for soap." According to a Nashville newspaper, most of the so-called loyal men of the South were "the merest trash that could be collected in a civilized community, of no personal credit or social responsibility." Thus, concludes a historian of reconstruction in Tennessee, "the power, wealth, culture, and natural leadership" of the state had been evicted from political control.[2] An upper-class Virginian sent Thad Stevens a bitter protest against being subjected to "our former slaves and the mean white surfs [*sic*] of the earth. . . . We are the children of the Lees, Clays, Henrys, Jeffersons and Jacksons. Tell me if we are to be ruled by these people." This would seem to suggest that to some extent and in some places southern class divisions were sharpened during the era of reconstruction. But southern conservatives exaggerated the degree to which the division between them and the radicals was along class lines.

In any case, those who have referred to the South's antebellum political rulers as its natural leaders are seldom explicit about what they mean. Remembering what had happened to the South under the guidance of her prewar politicians, it would be hard to argue that they had won the right to lead because they had governed so wisely or so well. If it is valid to judge statesmen by their understanding of the problems of their age, and by their efforts to find constructive solutions, the old southern leaders would have to be pronounced failures on both counts; and

---

[2] E. Merton Coulter: *William G. Brownlow* (Chapel Hill, 1937), pp. 282–3, 337.

many of them were, moreover, singularly irresponsible. Their strength was rooted in their economic power derived from large property holdings, and in their experience in the techniques of political manipulation. The conservatives' repeated complaint that the radicals paid no taxes and owned little property is highly suggestive, for their whole conception of natural political leadership ultimately boils down to this. When the radicals won control in the South, they did not displace a responsible political élite which had traditionally taken a large view of things; nor did they discharge a trained body of civil servants. This being the case, the change in leadership was far less disastrous than it has often been made to appear.

But the customary charges against the new southern leadership are extremely severe and need to be weighed carefully. It is essential, therefore, to examine in some detail each of the three elements in the radical coalition— the carpetbaggers, scalawags, and Negroes—to test the validity of the generalizations conservatives used to characterize them. The term "carpetbagger" was applied to recent northern settlers in the South who actively supported the radical Republicans.[3] Since the term has an invidious connotation, it is used here only for lack of another that is equally familiar but morally neutral. The so-called carpetbaggers were not all poor men who carried their meager possessions with them in carpetbags; they were not all ignorant; they were not all corrupt. Rather, they were a heterogeneous lot who moved to the South for a variety of reasons.

---

[3] "From contemporary usage . . . we derive the following as a nonvaluational definition: the men called carpetbaggers were *white Northerners who went south after the beginning of the Civil War and, sooner or later, became active in politics as Republicans.*" Richard N. Current: "Carpetbaggers Reconsidered," in *A Festschrift for Frederick B. Artz* (Durham, 1964), p. 144.

VI: *Radical Rule in the South*

Among the carpetbaggers were some who fitted the stereotype: disreputable opportunists and corruptionists who went south in search of political plunder or public office. Because these carpetbaggers were so conspicuous and gained such notoriety, conservative southern Democrats succeeded in portraying them as typical, though actually they constituted a small minority.

Few of the carpetbaggers came to the South originally for the purpose of entering politics; many of them arrived before 1867 when political careers were not even open to them. They migrated to the South in the same manner and for the same reasons that other Americans migrated to the West. They hoped to buy cotton lands or to enter legitimate business enterprises: to develop natural resources, build factories, promote railroads, represent insurance companies, or engage in trade. A large proportion of the carpetbaggers were veterans of the Union Army who were pleased with the southern climate and believed that they had discovered a land of opportunity. Others came as teachers, clergymen, officers of the Freedmen's Bureau, or agents of the various northern benevolent societies organized to give aid to the Negroes. These people went south to set up schools for Negroes and poor whites, to establish churches, and to distribute clothing and medical supplies. They were of all types—some well trained for their jobs, others not. Seldom, however, can they be dismissed as meddlesome fools, or can the genuineness of their humanitarian impulses be doubted. But whether honest or dishonest, northern settlers who became active in radical politics incurred the wrath of most white southern conservatives. For their supreme offense was not corruption but attempting to organize the Negroes for political action.

A scalawag is by definition a scamp, and white Southerners who collaborated with the radicals were thus stigmatized by the pejorative term that identified them. In southern society, according to one critic, scalawags constituted the "tory and deserter element, with a few from the obstructionists of the war time and malcontents of the present who wanted office."[4] But here, as in the case of the carpetbaggers, the facts were more complex than this. All scalawags were not degraded poor whites, depraved corruptionists, or cynical opportunists who betrayed the South for the spoils of office.

The cases of three distinguished scalawags will illustrate the inadequacy of any simple generalization about the character or origin of this class of radicals. The first is that of Lieutenant General James A. Longstreet of the Confederate Army, a graduate of West Point and one of Lee's ablest corps commanders. After the war Longstreet moved to New Orleans and became a partner in a cotton factorage business and head of an insurance firm. In 1867, arguing that the vanquished must accept the terms of the victors, he joined the Republican party and endorsed radical reconstruction. In 1868 he supported Grant for President, and in subsequent years Republican administrations gave him a variety of offices in the federal civil service. The second case is that of James L. Orr of South Carolina, a secessionist who had sat in the Confederate Senate. After serving as the Johnsonian governor of his state, Orr switched to the radicals and in 1868 was rewarded with a circuit judgeship. In a private letter he explained why he now supported the Republicans: It is "important for our prominent men to identify themselves with the radicals for the purpose of controlling their action and preventing mischief to the state." The third case is that of R. W.

---

[4] Walter L. Fleming: *Civil War and Reconstruction in Alabama* (New York, 1905), p. 402.

VI: *Radical Rule in the South*

Flournoy, a large slaveholder in ante-bellum Mississippi. Flournoy joined the radicals not for personal gain but because of a humanitarian interest in the welfare of the freedmen. In a letter to Stevens he once explained that he supported the Republicans as the party to whom the Negro "can alone look . . . for protection." Flournoy's support of racial equality made him one of the most hated scalawags in the state. None of these men fitted the scalawag stereotype.

Others unfortunately did. Among those who gave the scalawags their reputation for corruption was Franklin J. Moses, Jr., of South Carolina. The son of a distinguished father, Moses entered politics before the war and was known as an ardent secessionist. In 1867, after a brief period as a Johnsonian, he joined the radicals. Both as a legislator and, from 1872 to 1874, as governor he looted the public treasury and repeatedly accepted bribes for using his influence to secure the passage of legislation. Other scalawags appeared to be pure opportunists who simply joined the winning side. Joseph E. Brown, Georgia's Civil War governor, provides a classic example. After the war, claiming that he had sense enough to know when he was defeated, Brown quit the Democrats and urged Southerners to accept the radicals' terms. During the years of reconstruction, in addition to his political activities, he found the time (and the opportunity) to become a wealthy capitalist: president of a railroad, a steamship company, a coal company, and an iron company. When the radicals were overthrown in Georgia, Brown, as always, landed on his feet and returned to the Democratic party. Now he helped to organize a powerful Democratic machine that dominated the state for many years and eventually sent him to the United States Senate.

Always a minority of the southern white population,

more numerous in some states than in others,[5] the scalawags usually belonged to one or more of four distinct
groups. The first and largest of these groups was the
Unionists. Having been exposed to severe persecution
from their Confederate neighbors during the war, southern Unionists were often the most vindictive of the radicals; they were quite willing to support those who would
now retaliate against the secessionists, and they hoped that
congressional reconstruction would give them political
control in their states. Early in 1866 a North Carolinian
wrote Stevens that Union men were disillusioned with
Johnson but still hoped "that traitors will be punished
for the treatment that union men received at their hands."

However, a very large proportion of this Unionist-scala-
wag element had little enthusiasm for one aspect of the
radical program: the granting of equal civil and political
rights to the Negroes. They favored the disenfranchisement of the Confederates to enable them to dominate the
new state governments, but they were reluctant to accept
Negro suffrage. "There is some small amount of squirm-
ing about the privileges extended to the recent slaves," a
Virginia Unionist informed Stevens, "but time will overcome all this as there is no union man who does not infinitely more fear and dread the domination of the recent
Rebels than that of the recent slaves." In 1866, General
Clinton B. Fisk, an officer of the Freedmen's Bureau, told
the congressional Committee on Reconstruction that in
Tennessee "among the bitterest opponents of the negro
. . . are the intensely radical loyalists of the [eastern]

---

[5] In the presidential election of 1872, according to a recent estimate,
approximately 150,000 white Southerners voted Republican; they
constituted about 20 per cent of the white voters. These scalawags
were most numerous in Tennessee, North Carolina, Arkansas, Texas,
and Virginia. Allen W. Trelease: "Who Were the Scalawags?"
Journal of Southern History, XXIX (1963), p. 458.

mountain districts. . . . The great opposition to the measure in the Tennessee legislature, giving the negro the right to testify and an equality before the law, has come from that section, chiefly. In Middle Tennessee and in West Tennessee the largest and the wealthiest planters . . . have more cordially cooperated with me in my duties than the people of East Tennessee." The planters believed that they could control the Negro vote, and the scalawags feared that they would.

Insofar as there was any relationship between scalawags and the class structure of the South, it resulted from the fact that a minority of the poor whites and yeoman farmers were attracted to the radical cause.[6] There had always been, as we have seen, an undercurrent of tension between them and the planter class, and some of them deserted President Johnson when it appeared that his program would return the planters to power. Lower-class whites who joined the radicals sometimes hoped for a seizure of the planters' lands. In South Carolina, according to a Union officer, the idea of confiscation "was received with more favor by this caste than by the Negroes." He recalled numerous occasions when "dirty, ragged, stupid creatures slyly inquired of me, 'When is our folks a-gwine to git the lan'?' " But it was never easy for the yeomen or poor whites to become scalawags, for support of the radicals meant collaboration with Negroes, or at least acquiescence in Negro suffrage. As a result, this class of scalawags was most numerous in areas with a small Negro population. Elsewhere a few lower-class whites managed to submerge their race prejudice, but the great majority preferred the old conservative leadership to a party that seemed to preach equality of the races.

---

[6] Most of the lower-class whites who became scalawags had been Unionists, but some had supported the Confederacy.

A third source of scalawag strength came from Southerners engaged in business enterprise and from those living in regions, such as East Tennessee, western Virginia and North Carolina, and northern Alabama, which were rich in natural resources and had an industrial potential. Among such men there was considerable support for the economic policies of the Republican party—for the national banking system, the protective tariff, and federal appropriations for internal improvements. In general, the radical governments invited northern capitalists to invest in the South, granted loans or subsidies to the railroads, and gave charters and franchises to new corporations. Some of the scalawags were thus identified with the concept of a New South whose economy would be more diversified than that of the Old.

Finally, the radicals drew a little of their scalawag support and some of their leaders from upper-class Southerners who had been affiliated with the Whig party before the Civil War. The Whig party had been particularly attractive to the more affluent and socially secure members of southern society, and after the war many Whigs were reluctant to join their old foes, the Democrats. A few of them now looked upon the Republican party as the heir to the Whig tradition and wondered whether it might be possible not only to join but also to control its organization in the South. Upper-class Whig scalawags found it relatively easy to accept equal civil and political rights for Negroes, first, because among them race hatred was less often the prime motivating force of political action and, second, because they were optimistic about their chances of controlling the Negro vote. In Mississippi, for example, James L. Alcorn, elected governor on the Republican ticket in 1869, had been a prominent Whig planter before the war, as had been numerous other leading scalawags.

VI: *Radical Rule in the South*

Thus it would appear that the scalawags were in part an absurd coalition of class-conscious poor whites and yeoman farmers who hated the planters, and class-conscious Whig planters and businessmen who disliked the egalitarian Democrats. But politics has a logic of its own, and the history of American political parties is full of contradictions such as this.

Joining the carpetbaggers and scalawags in the radical coalition was the mass of southern Negroes, most of them illiterate, many easily intimidated. Because of their political inexperience and economic helplessness, they were sometimes misled and victimized not only by Republicans but also by southern white Democrats. But it would be far from the truth to say that their political behavior during reconstruction was altogether passive or irresponsible. This was untrue, if for no other reason, because the issues of reconstruction, so far as the Negroes were concerned, were relatively simple and clear-cut. Given their condition and the limited political choices open to them, most Negroes responded to the appeals of rival politicians in a manner that had an obvious logic to it.

To begin with, suffrage was not something thrust upon an indifferent mass of Negroes. Their leaders had demanded it from the start; and when the Johnson governments limited the ballot to the whites, many meetings of southern Negroes sent protests to Congress. In Tennessee, for example, Negroes first petitioned the legislature for the ballot, then asked Congress not to seat Tennesseans until their petition was granted. On May 7, 1866, a meeting of freedmen in New Bern, North Carolina, resolved "That so long as the Federal Government refuses to grant us the right to protect ourselves by means of the ballot . . . we will hold it responsible before God for our protection."

Moreover, most Negroes fully appreciated the importance of achieving literacy, and they took advantage of the limited educational opportunities offered them with almost pathetic eagerness. They also understood that in the rural South land was the key to economic independence and that they needed government aid to get it. In 1865 they heard rumors that Congress would provide each of them with forty acres and a mule at Christmas time; the next year they heard the same rumors again; once more in 1867 they hoped to get land when the radicals formulated their reconstruction program. But each time the Negroes were disappointed, and by 1868 they knew that the Republicans in Congress were not going to assist them.

Nevertheless, an overwhelming majority of Negro voters continued to support the Republican party, and in 1868 they helped to elevate General Grant to the presidency. In the political campaigns of the reconstruction era, Democratic candidates occasionally tried to bid for the Negro vote, but the record of the Johnson governments and the commitment of the Democratic party to white supremacy caused the mass of Negroes to remain loyal Republicans. "The blacks know that many conservatives hope to reduce them again to some form of peonage," a Tennessee carpetbagger wrote Stevens. "Under the impulse of this fear they will roll up their whole strength . . . and will go entirely for the Republican candidate whoever he may be." As long as southern Democrats opposed Negro suffrage and insisted that white supremacy was the central political issue, this condition could hardly have changed. It was this that made it easy for the agents of the Republican Union League to mobilize and "control" the Negro vote. Yet white Democrats often cited this solid Negro support of the Republicans to illustrate the political irresponsibility of the freedmen. It was a curious argument, however, for the practical choice offered the Negro voters was between a party that gave them civil and political rights and a party whose stock-in-trade was racist demagoguery.

Perhaps the most important generalizations to be made about the role of the Negroes in reconstruction are the following. First, while they had influence in all of the southern radical governments—more in some than in others—they did not control any of them. They served in all of the state legislatures, but only in South Carolina, one of the two southern states in which they outnumbered the whites, were they in the majority.[7] In Mississippi, the other state in which the Negroes had a numerical majority, the carpetbaggers controlled politics; while in Tennessee, where the scalawags dominated the radical government, there were practically no Negro officeholders at all. Few Negroes were elected to higher offices; none became the governor of a state. At various times South Carolina had a Negro lieutenant governor, secretary of state, treasurer, speaker of the house, and associate justice of the state supreme court; Mississippi had a Negro lieutenant governor, secretary of state, superintendent of education, and speaker of the house; Louisiana had a Negro lieutenant governor, secretary of state, treasurer, and superintendent of public education; Florida had a Negro secretary of state, and superintendent of public instruction. Nearly all of them were men of ability and integrity. Fourteen Negroes were elected to the United States House of Representatives, six of them from South Carolina. Two Mississippi Negroes served in the United States Senate: Hiram R. Revels for a one-year unexpired term, and Blanche K. Bruce for a full term. (Revels and Bruce, incidentally, are

---

[7] South Carolina's first radical legislature contained 87 Negroes and 69 whites. The Negroes, however, had a majority only in the lower house. The upper house contained twice as many whites as Negroes.

the only Negroes who have ever been elected to the Senate from any state, North or South.) In general, however, white men dominated the higher offices of the southern radical governments. The Negroes, though filling many city and county offices, ordinarily were unable to advance beyond the state legislatures.

Second, the Negroes soon developed their own leadership and were not always the mere tools of white Republicans. In 1868 a Florida carpetbagger reported to Stevens that white radicals were having trouble getting the Negroes to support ratification of the new state constitution. "The colored preachers," he wrote, "are *the great power* in controlling and uniting the colored vote, and they are looked to, as political leaders, with more confidence . . . than to any other source of instruction and control." Some of the Negro leaders were corruptible, some incorruptible; some had great ability, some little. Most of them were conservatives on all issues except civil and political rights.

Finally, the Negroes were seldom vindictive in their use of political power or in their attitude toward native whites. To be sure, there were plenty of cases of friction between Negroes and whites, and Negro militiamen were sometimes inordinately aggressive. But in no southern state did any responsible Negro leader, or any substantial Negro group, attempt to get complete political control into the hands of the freedmen.[8] All they asked for was equal political rights and equality before the law. Thus, in 1866, a group of North Carolina Negroes in thanking Congress for the Civil Rights Act promised that "whenever the Elective Franchise is also guaranteed to us we will ask no further special protection from the Federal Government, for then united with our white friends in the

---

[8] However, Negro leaders did protest when they thought that white radicals were trying to monopolize the offices.

South we will be able to secure for ourselves every desired or desirable means of prosperity." Negroes did not desire to have political parties divided along racial lines; rather, unlike most white Democrats, they were eager to drop the race issue and work with the whites within the existing party framework.

Many Negroes at this time were even willing to postpone action on social segregation, especially in the schools, preferring to avoid conflict over this issue while they concentrated on civil and political rights. A South Carolina Negro legislator declared: "I venture to say to my white fellow-citizens that we, the colored people, are not in quest of social equality. I for one do not ask to be introduced in your family circle if you are not disposed to receive me there." And yet a northern white conservative affirmed that in South Carolina radical reconstruction "is barbarism overwhelming civilization by physical force. It is the slave rioting in the halls of his master, and putting that master under his feet." Such a description should be taken for what it was: the hyperbole of partisan politics.

The first step in the organization of new southern state governments, as required by the reconstruction acts, was the election of delegates to conventions to frame new state constitutions. Since these conventions were controlled by the radicals, since they were the first political bodies in the South to contain Negroes,[9] white conservatives subjected them to violent denunciation. They contemptu-

---

[9] The number of Negroes and whites in the various conventions was as follows:

	Negro	White		Negro	White
ALABAMA	18	90	MISSISSIPPI	16	84
ARKANSAS	8	58	NORTH CAROLINA	15	118
FLORIDA	18	27	SOUTH CAROLINA	76	48
GEORGIA	33	137	VIRGINIA	25	80
LOUISIANA	49	49	TEXAS	9	81

ously called them "black and tan conventions"; they described the delegates as "baboons, monkeys, mules," or "ragamuffins and jailbirds." The South Carolina convention, according to a local newspaper, was the "maddest, most infamous revolution in history."

Yet, the invectives notwithstanding, there was nothing mad and little revolutionary about the work of these conventions.[1] In fact, one of the most significant observations to be made about them is that the delegates showed little interest in experimentation. For the most part the radicals wrote orthodox state constitutions, borrowing heavily from the previous constitutions and from those of other states. To find fault with the way these southern constitutions were drawn is to find fault with the way most new state constitutions have been drawn; to criticize their basic political structure is to criticize the basic political structure of all the states. They were neither original nor unique. There was no inclination to test, say, the unicameral legislature, or novel executive or judicial systems.

Nor did the conventions attempt radical experiments in the field of social or economic policy. Since land reform had been defeated in Congress, a few delegates tried to achieve it through state action. The South Carolina convention provided for the creation of a commission to purchase land for sale to Negroes. In Louisiana, some Negro delegates proposed that when planters sold their estates purchases of more than 150 acres be prohibited. One white scalawag suggested a double tax on uncultivated land. A few delegates in other states advocated various policies designed to force the breakup of large estates. But

---

[1] The Democrats accused the Republican delegates of wasting time and of extravagance. The printing bills of some of these conventions were unnecessarily high, but in general these accusations have relatively little evidence to support them.

these and all other attacks upon landed property were easily defeated.

As for the freedmen, the new constitutions proclaimed the equality of all men by quoting or paraphrasing the Declaration of Independence. Negroes were given the same civil and political rights as white men. "The equality of all persons before the law," proclaimed the Arkansas constitution, "is recognized and shall ever remain inviolate; nor shall any citizen ever be deprived of any right, privilege, or immunity, nor exempted from any burden or duty, on account of race, color, or previous condition." But on the subject of the social relations of Negroes and whites, most of the radical constitutions were evasive. South Carolina provided that its public schools were to be open to all "without regard to race or color," but only the state university actually made an attempt at integration. The Louisiana constitution declared: "There shall be no separate schools or institutions of learning established exclusively for any race by the State of Louisiana." In New Orleans from 1871 to 1877 about one third of the public schools were integrated, and white resistance was remarkably mild; but elsewhere in Louisiana segregation was the rule. Outside of South Carolina and Louisiana the radicals made no explicit constitutional provision for social integration. The Mississippi convention first defeated a proposal that segregated schools be required, then defeated a proposal that they be prohibited; the result was that the new constitution ignored the issue altogether. The only reference to segregation in it was a vague statement that "the rights of all citizens to travel upon public conveyances shall not be infringed upon, nor in any manner abridged in this state." But whether or not this clause prohibited segregation in public transportation is far from clear.

The Era of Reconstruction

Yet, though the new constitutions were essentially conservative documents, they did accomplish some modest reforms, most of which were long overdue. In general, they eliminated certain undemocratic features of the old constitutions, for example, the inequitable systems of legislative apportionment that had discriminated against the interior regions of Virginia, North Carolina, and South Carolina. In the states of the Southeast, many offices that had previously been appointive were now made elective, and county government was taken out of the hands of local oligarchies. The rights of women were enlarged, tax systems were made more equitable, penal codes were reformed, and the number of crimes punishable by death was reduced. Most of the constitutions provided for substantial improvements in the state systems of public education and in the facilities for the care of the physically and mentally handicapped and of the poor.[2]

In South Carolina, according to the historians of reconstruction in that state, the radical convention was an orderly body which accomplished its work with reasonable dispatch. It produced a constitution "as good as any other constitution that state has ever had"—good enough to remain in force for nearly two decades after the white Democrats regained control. This was, in fact, the state's first really democratic constitution; for, in addition to removing distinctions based on race, it provided for manhood suffrage, abolished property qualifications for officeholding, gave the voters the power for the first time to select the governor and other state officers, and transferred the

---

[2] Attempts to accomplish a sweeping disenfranchisement of Confederate sympathizers were defeated either in the conventions or, as in Virginia and Mississippi, by popular vote. The disenfranchisement accomplished by these constitutions seldom went beyond those disqualified for holding office by the Fourteenth Amendment, and all made provision for the eventual restoration of the franchise even to them.

election of presidential electors from the legislature to the voters. Another important provision related to public education: unlike the previous constitution, "the fundamental law of the state carried the obligation of universal education" and aimed at "the creation of a school system like that of Northern states." Other reforms included an extension of women's rights, adoption of the state's first divorce law, strengthening of the state's fiscal power, revision of the tax system, and modernization of the judiciary and of county government.[3]

The responsible behavior of South Carolina's radical constitutional convention was in striking contrast to the angry and irresponsible criticism of the Democrats. Chiefly because of its provisions for racial equality, they ridiculed the new constitution as "the work of sixty-odd negroes, many of them ignorant and depraved, together with fifty white men, outcasts of Northern society, and Southern renegades, betrayers of their race and country." Specifically, the Democrats charged that manhood suffrage was designed to further the ambitions of "mean whites"; that Negro suffrage would bring ruin to the state; that the judicial reforms were "repugnant to our customs and habits of thought"; and that the public school requirements were "a fruitful source of peculant corruption." In spite of this fanciful criticism by a party whose chief appeal was to racial bigotry, the work of the radical convention was ratified by a majority of nearly three to one.

At the time that the new constitutions were ratified, elections were held for state officers and legislators. After the elections, when Congress approved of the constitutions, political power was transferred from the military to the new civil governments. Thus began the era of radical

---

[3] Francis B. Simkins and Robert H. Woody: *South Carolina during Reconstruction* (Chapel Hill, 1932), pp. 90–111.

government in the South—an era which, according to tradition, produced some of the worst state administrations
in American history. Some of the southern radical regimes earned their evil reputations, others did not; but
viewed collectively, there was much in the record they
made to justify severe criticism. To say that they were not
always models of efficiency and integrity would be something of an understatement. "The great impediment of
the Republican party in this state," wrote a Tennessee
radical, "is the incompetence of its leaders. . . . After the
war the loyal people in many counties had no competent
men to be judges, lawyers or political leaders." Indeed, all
of the radical governments suffered more or less from the
incompetence of some, the dishonesty of a few, and above
all the inexperience of most of the officeholders. Unques-
tionably the poorest records were made in South Carolina
during the administrations of the carpetbagger Robert K.
Scott and the scalawag Franklin J. Moses, Jr., and in Louisiana during the administrations of the carpetbaggers
Henry C. Warmoth and William P. Kellogg.

The sins of various radical governments included fraudulent bond issues; graft in land sales or purchases and in
the letting of contracts for public works; and waste and
extravagance in the use of state funds. Governor Warmoth
was reputed to have pocketed $100,000 during his first
year in office, though his salary was $8,000; another gov-
ernor was accused of stealing and selling the supplies of
the Freedmen's Bureau. A scalawag governor admitted
taking bribes of more than $40,000; another fraudulently
endorsed state bonds over to a group of railroad promoters. In Louisiana under both Warmoth and Kellogg there
was corruption in the granting of charters and franchises,
in the negotiation of construction contracts, in the use of
school funds, in the collection of state taxes, and in the

Failures ↓

awarding of printing contracts. Some of the radical legislators, especially in South Carolina, apparently made bribery an integral part of the process of transacting legislative business. One South Carolina legislature issued bonds valued at $1,590,000 to redeem bank notes valued at $500,000; it voted a bonus of $1,000 to the speaker when he lost that amount in a bet on a horse race. For a time the legislators of this state enjoyed the services of a free restaurant and bar established for their private use; they billed the state for such "legislative supplies" as hams, ladies' bonnets, perfumes, champagne, and (for one unfortunate member) a coffin. The cost of state printing in South Carolina between 1868 and 1876 was greater than the cost had been from 1789 to 1868. On one occasion, as the legislature was about to adjourn, a Democratic newspaper in Charleston wrote the following epitaph: "In life it has been unlovely, and in death it has not belied its record. As it lived, it has died—an uncouth, malformed and abortive monstrosity, its birth a blunder, its life a crime, and its death a blessing."

Debt + Tax

Meanwhile, the credit of some of the southern states was impaired as public debts mounted. In Florida the state debt increased from $524,000 in 1868 to $5,621,000 in 1874. In South Carolina a legislative committee reported that between 1868 and 1871 the state debt had increased from $5,403,000 to $15,768,000, but another committee insisted that it had increased to $29,159,000. By 1872 the debts of the eleven states of the former Confederacy had increased by approximately $132,000,000. The burden on taxpayers grew apace. Between 1860 and 1870 South Carolina's tax rate more than doubled, while property values declined by more than fifty per cent. In Tennessee a radical reported that during the first three years after the war taxes had increased sevenfold, though property had de-

Tax + Debt

clined in value by one third. Throughout the South the tax burden was four times as great in 1870 as it had been in 1860. Such rates, complained many southern land-holders, were confiscatory; and, indeed, taxes and other adversities of the postwar years forced some of them to sell all or part of their lands. Sympathy for South Carolina's planter aristocracy caused a northern conservative to ask: "When before did mankind behold the spectacle of a rich, high-spirited, cultivated, self-governed people suddenly cast down, bereft of their possessions, and put under the feet of the slaves they had held in bondage for centuries?"

Defense of Gov'ts

High taxes, mounting debts, corruption, extravagance, and waste, however, do not constitute the complete record of the radical regimes. Moreover, to stop with a mere de-scription of their misdeeds would be to leave all the cru-cial questions unanswered—to distort the picture and to view it without perspective. For example, if some of these governments contained an uncommonly large number of inexperienced or incompetent officeholders, if much of their support came from an untutored electorate, there was an obvious reason for this. Howard K. Beale, in a cri-tique of various reconstruction legends, observed that the political rulers of the ante-bellum South "had fastened ig-norance or inexperience on millions of whites as well as Negroes and that it was this ignorance and inexperience that caused trouble when Radicals were in power. . . . Wealthy Southerners . . . seldom recognized the need for general education of even the *white* masses."[4] Even in 1865 the men who won control of the Johnson govern-ments showed little disposition to adopt the needed re-forms. In South Carolina the Johnsonians did almost nothing to establish a system of public education, and at

---

[4] Howard K. Beale: "On Rewriting Reconstruction History," *American Historical Review*, XLV (1940), pp. 807–27.

Defense

the time that the radicals came to power only one eighth of the white children of school age were attending school. The Negroes, of course, had been ignored entirely. It was probably no coincidence that the radicals made their poorest record in South Carolina, the state which had done the least for education and whose prewar government had been the least democratic.

As for the corruption of the radical governments, this phenomenon can be understood only when it is related to the times and to conditions throughout the country. One must remember that the administrations of President Grant set the moral tone for American government at all levels, national, state, and local. The best-remembered episodes of the Grant era are its numerous scandals—the Crédit Mobilier and the Whiskey Ring being the most spectacular of them—involving members of Congress as well as men in high administration circles. There were, moreover, singularly corrupt Republican machines in control of various northern states, including Massachusetts, New York, and Pennsylvania. But corruption was not a phenomenon peculiar to Republicans of the Gilded Age, as the incredible operations of the so-called Tweed Ring in New York City will testify. Indeed, the thefts of public funds by this organization of white Tammany Democrats surpassed the total thefts in all the southern states combined.

Clearly the presence of carpetbaggers, scalawags, and Negroes in the radical governments was not in itself a sufficient explanation for the appearance of corruption. The South was being affected by the same forces that were affecting the rest of the country. No doubt the most important of these forces were, first, the social disorganization that accompanied the Civil War and hit the defeated and demoralized South with particular severity; and, second,

Defense

the frantic economic expansion of the postwar period, when the American economy was dominated by a group of extraordinarily talented but irresponsible and undisciplined business leaders. These entrepreneurs' rather flexible standards of public morality provided an unfortunate model for the politicians.

Whether southern Democrats would have been able to resist the corrupting forces of the postwar decade had they remained in power is by no means certain. Perhaps the old ruling class would have been somewhat less vulnerable to the temptations of the Gilded Age, but the record of the Johnson governments was spotty at best. In Louisiana the conservative government created by Lincoln and Johnson wasted a great deal of public money. In Mississippi the state treasurer of the Johnson government embezzled $62,000. (This, by the way, far surpassed the record of the only thief in the radical government, who embezzled $7,000.) E. Merton Coulter discovered that during the era of reconstruction some Democratic officeholders "partook of the same financial characteristics as Radicals" and "took advantage of openings" when they found them. He quotes a Georgia editor who claimed that the extravagance and corruption "benefitted about as many Democrats as Republicans"; and he notes that a Democratic administration in Alabama "in lack of honesty differed little from the administrations of the Radicals between whom it was sandwiched."[5]

In the 1870's, when the South's so-called "natural leaders" returned to power, that troubled section did not always find itself governed by politicians distinguished for their selfless devotion to public service. In Mississippi the treasurer of the Democratic regime that overthrew the radicals in 1875 immediately embezzled $316,000, which

---

[5] Coulter, *The South during Reconstruction*, pp. 152-3.

broke all previous records! Elsewhere in the next decade eight other state treasurers were guilty of defalcations or embezzlements, including one in Louisiana who defrauded the state of more than a million dollars. Georgia was now ruled by a Democratic machine that was both ruthless and corrupt, a machine whose record was so offensive that by the end of the 1880's the white masses—some even willing to accept Negro support—rose in political rebellion against it. Reports about the Mississippi Democratic regime of the late nineteenth century are particularly colorful. One white editor charged that an "infamous ring" of "corrupt office-seekers . . . [had] debauched the ballot boxes . . . incurred useless and extravagant expenditures, raised the taxes, [and] plunged the State into debt." At the Mississippi constitutional convention of 1890, a white Democratic delegate gave the following description of politics in his state during the previous fifteen years: "Sir, it is no secret that there has not been a full vote and a fair count in Mississippi since 1875. . . . In other words we have been stuffing ballot boxes, committing perjury, and here and there in the state carrying the elections by fraud and violence. . . . No man can be in favor of perpetuating the election methods which have prevailed in Mississippi since 1875 who is not a moral idiot." Twelve years later an editor claimed that it would tax "the range and scope of the most fertile and versatile imagination to picture a condition of greater political rottenness" than existed in Mississippi at that time.

In the final analysis the crucial question about the extravagance and peculations of the radical governments is who the chief beneficiaries were. Only a few of the Negro and white radical leaders profited personally. The funds they stole, the money that prodigal legislators used for their own benefit, accounted for only a small fraction of the increased debts of the southern states. Nor did the total sums involved in bribery rise to a very impressive figure. And why was the tar brush applied exclusively to those who accepted the bribes and not to those who offered them? Under these circumstances is it really more blessed to give than to receive? For when the bribe-givers are identified we have located those who profited most from radical misdeeds. These men were the construction contractors, business speculators, and railroad promoters, or their agents, who hoped to persuade legislators to give them contracts, franchises, charters, subsidies, financial grants, or guarantees. They were the men who were also corrupting Congressmen and northern legislatures.

In Virginia much of the history of reconstruction concerns the rivalry of the Baltimore and Ohio Railroad and the Southside line for control of the Virginia and Tennessee Railroad. Both lines fought to control elections and legislators and backed whichever party promised to serve them, until, in 1870, the legislature ended the dispute by approving the consolidation plans of the Southside. Louisiana's reconstruction politics was enlivened by the attempt of a railroad and steamship corporation, headed by Charles Morgan of New York, to prevent the state from subsidizing a rival line between New Orleans and Houston, until Morgan forced the new line to take him in. In Alabama the North and South Railroad and the Alabama and Chattanooga Railroad battled for access to the ore deposits around Birmingham. In the process the competing groups corrupted both Johnson and radical legislatures, and in the latter both Republicans and Democrats.

Most of the debt increases in the southern states resulted not from the thefts and extravagance of radical legislators but from the grants and guarantees they gave to railroad promoters, among whom were always some native white

Democrats. In Florida more than sixty per cent of the debt incurred by the radical regime was in the form of railroad guarantee bonds. In North Carolina the radical government, prodded by the carpetbagger Milton S. Littlefield, a skilled lobbyist, issued millions of dollars of railroad bonds. Among those who benefited were many of the state's "best citizens," including George W. Swepson, a local business promoter and Democrat. Most of Alabama's reconstruction debt—$18,000,000 out of $20,500,000—was in the form of state bonds issued to subsidize railroad construction, for which the state obtained liens upon railroad property. When one measure for state aid was before the Alabama legislature, many Democrats were among the lobbyists working for its passage. Yet, complained a radical, the Democrats who expect to profit from the bill "will use the argument that the Republican party had a majority in the Legislature, and will falsely, but hopefully, charge it upon Republicans as a partisan crime against the state."

Indeed, all of the southern states, except Mississippi, used state credit to finance the rebuilding and expansion of their railroads, for private sources of credit were inadequate. This policy had been developed before the war; it was continued under the Johnsonians; and in some cases when the Democrats overthrew the radicals there was no decline in the state's generosity to the railroads. While the radicals controlled the southern legislatures, not only they but many members of the Democratic minority as well voted for railroad bond issues. According to an historian of reconstruction in Louisiana, "Such measures were supported by members of both parties, often introduced by Democrats, in every case supported by a large majority of Democrats in both houses."[6] The subservience of many

---

[6] Ella Lonn: *Reconstruction in Louisiana after 1868* (New York, 1918), pp. 36–7.

postwar southern legislatures to the demands of railroad and other business promoters is in some respects less shocking than pathetic. For it expressed a kind of blind faith shared by many Southerners of both parties that railroad building and industrialization would swiftly solve all of their section's problems. No price seemed too high for such a miracle.

In several states, for obviously partisan reasons, the actual increase in the size of the public debt was grossly exaggerated. In Mississippi, for example, there was a durable legend among white Democrats that the radicals had added $20,000,000 to the state debt, when, in fact, they added only $500,000. Mississippi radicals had guarded against extravagance by inserting a clause in the constitution of 1868 prohibiting the pledging of state funds to aid private corporations—a clause which the conservatives, incidentally, had opposed. In Alabama, apart from railroad bonds secured by railroad property, the radicals added only $2,500,000 to the state debt. They did not leave a debt of $30,000,000 as conservatives claimed. In most other states, when loans to the railroads are subtracted, the increases in state debts for which the radicals were responsible appear far less staggering.

As for taxes, one of the positive achievements of many of the radical governments was the adoption of more equitable tax systems which put a heavier burden upon the planters. Before the war the southern state governments had performed few public services and the tax burden on the landed class had been negligible; hence the vehement protests of the landholders were sometimes as much against radical tax policies as against the alleged waste of taxpayers' money. The restoration governments often brought with them a return to the old inequitable fiscal systems. In Mississippi the subsequent claim of the conservatives that they had reduced the tax burden the radicals had placed upon property holders was quite misleading. The conservatives did lower the state property tax, but, as a consequence, they found it necessary to shift various services and administrative burdens from the state to the counties. This led to an increase in the cost of county government, an increase in the rate of county taxes, and a net increase in total taxes, state and county, that Mississippi property holders had to pay.

As a matter of fact, taxes, government expenditures, and public debts were bound to increase in the southern states during the postwar years no matter who controlled them. For there was no way to escape the staggering job of physical reconstruction—the repair of public buildings, bridges, and roads—and costs had started to go up under the Johnson governments before the radicals came to power. So far from the expenditures of the reconstruction era being totally lost in waste and fraud, much of this physical reconstruction was accomplished while the radicals were in office. They expanded the state railroad systems, increased public services, and provided public school systems—in some states for the first time. Since schools and other public services were now provided for Negroes as well as for whites, a considerable increase in the cost of state government could hardly have been avoided. In Florida between 1869 and 1873 the number of children enrolled in the public schools trebled; in South Carolina between 1868 and 1876 the number increased from 30,000 to 123,000. The economies achieved by some of the restoration governments came at the expense of the schools and various state institutions such as hospitals for the insane. The southern propertied classes had always been reluctant to tax themselves to support education or state hospitals, and in many cases the budget-cutting of the conservatives simply strangled them.

Thus radical rule, in spite of its shortcomings, was by

no means synonymous with incompetence and corruption; far too many carpetbagger, scalawag, and Negro politicians made creditable records to warrant such a generalization. Moreover, conditions were improving in the final years of reconstruction. In South Carolina the last radical administration, that of the carpetbagger Governor Daniel H. Chamberlain, was dedicated to reform; in Florida "the financial steadiness of the state government increased toward the end of Republican rule."[7] In Mississippi the radicals made a remarkably good record. The first radical governor, James L. Alcorn, a scalawag, was a man of complete integrity; the second, Adelbert Ames, a carpetbagger, was honest, able, and sincerely devoted to protecting the rights of the Negroes. Mississippi radicals, according to Vernon L. Wharton, established a system of public education far better than any the state had known before; reorganized the state judiciary and adopted a new code of laws; renovated public buildings and constructed new ones, including state hospitals at Natchez and Vicksburg; and provided better state asylums for the blind, deaf, and dumb. The radicals, Wharton concludes, gave Mississippi "a government of greatly expanded functions at a cost that was low in comparison with that of almost any other state."[8] No major political scandal occurred in Mississippi during the years of radical rule—indeed, it was the best governed state in the postwar South. Yet white conservatives attacked the radical regime in Mississippi as violently as they did in South Carolina, which suggests that their basic grievance was not corruption but race policy.

Finally, granting all their mistakes, the radical governments were by far the most democratic the South had ever

---

[7] William W. Davis: *The Civil War and Reconstruction in Florida* (New York, 1913), pp. 672–3.
[8] Wharton, *The Negro in Mississippi,* pp. 179–80.

known. They were the only governments in southern history to extend to Negroes complete civil and political equality, and to try to protect them in the enjoyment of the rights they were granted. The overthrow of these governments was hardly a victory for political democracy, for the conservatives who "redeemed" the South tried to relegate poor men, Negro and white, once more to political obscurity. Near the end of the nineteenth century another battle for political democracy would have to be waged; but this time it would be, for the most part, a more limited version—for whites only. As for the Negroes, they would have to struggle for another century to regain what they had won—and then lost—in the years of radical reconstruction.

CHAPTER SEVEN

Triumph of the Conservatives

The year 1876, the centennial of American independence, had special meaning for southern white Democrats. This was the year when they fought the last great
battle with the radical Republicans; when, in the folklore of the white South, a new generation of Minute Men
engaged in another heroic struggle to throw off the yoke
of tyranny and oppression. Eight of the southern states
had already fallen to the Democrats,[1] but three of them—
South Carolina, Florida, and Louisiana—were still in the
hands of the coalition of carpetbaggers, scalawags, and Negroes. In the elections of 1876, the Democrats claimed to
have won these remaining states; and the new President,
Rutherford B. Hayes, though a Republican, was not
inclined to dispute the point. In April 1877, Hayes withdrew the last federal troops from the South and surrendered political control of South Carolina, Florida, and
Louisiana to the Democrats.

The South was "redeemed." This favorite euphemism
of the white Democrats meant that the federal government
had renounced responsibility for reconstruction, aban-

---

[1] The Democrats won control of Tennessee in 1869; of Virginia and
North Carolina in 1870; of Georgia in 1871; of Alabama, Arkansas,
and Texas in 1874; and of Mississippi in 1875.

doned the Negro, and, in effect, invited southern white men to formulate their own program of political, social, and economic readjustment. These developments were by no means the least of the tragedies of the so-called "tragic era." How they came about remains to be explained.

The first sign of what might ultimately happen was the decision of the Republicans in 1868 to nominate Ulysses S. Grant for the presidency—to pass over all of the recognized Republican leaders in favor of a popular military hero who would appeal to the less committed and more practical elements in the party. Grant lacked the moral dedication that was so vital an element in Republican radicalism; in fact, he had been a conservative until Johnson had pushed him into the arms of the radicals. He failed to provide the firm leadership that was essential in a period of profound social change. In spite of his good intentions, he contributed little but political ineptitude. Worst of all, he filled his Cabinet with mediocrities and party hacks, some of whom helped to give the Gilded Age its shabby reputation.

The inauguration of Grant marked the approaching end of the Republican party's creative role as the political instrument of what Charles A. Beard has called "The Second American Revolution."[2] Since its birth in the 1850's this party had been a dynamic force in the political, social, and economic life of the United States. It had sponsored the policies which hastened the triumph of an urban-industrial social order over the already declining rural-agrarian interests centered in the South and West: the protective tariff; a new national banking system; a sound paper currency in national bank notes secured by government

---

[2] The label that Beard gave to the years of the Civil War and reconstruction is quite appropriate, but it implies more than his narrow concentration on economic change.

bonds; a prohibitive federal tax on the note issues of irresponsible state banks; federal subsidies for internal improvements, especially for the railroads; the sale of mineral and timber resources on the public domain to private enterprise; and finally, in 1869, an act providing that federal securities, most of which had been purchased during the war with depreciated paper money, were to be redeemed in gold. Having achieved all this, the Republican party's economic role became less dynamic—more one of consolidation, of defending policies already in force against the criticism of discontented groups, especially farmers and urban workers. Thus, on questions of economic policy, Republicans began to find themselves on the defensive rather than on the attack.

Their southern policy, too, was now almost completed. They had crushed the secession movement, restored the Union, and vindicated American nationality. They had destroyed the Calhoun conception of state sovereignty— never again would a group of disaffected states contemplate disunion as a potential remedy—and the trend toward expanding federal power went on relentlessly. Republicans had permanently reduced the enormous political influence that the South had enjoyed before the war. They had achieved the abolition of slavery, written guarantees of civil and political rights for Negroes into the federal Constitution, and fully developed a program of political reconstruction. By 1869 land reform was a dead issue, and the Freedmen's Bureau began to wind up its affairs. Thus Republicans disavowed further federal responsibility for the Negro's economic future, or for providing him with educational opportunities. Here, too, future Republican policy would be one of retrenchment, of consolidation, not one of continuing development. Practical Republicans still found the votes of Negroes useful, and

VII: *Triumph of the Conservatives*

until the mid-seventies they continued to support the southern radical governments as best they could. But radical reconstruction was clearly entering a period of decline, and the constructive role of the Republican party in the remaking of the South was nearly finished.

These changes in the character and function of the party were accompanied by the decay and rapid disappearance from public life of the old radical leadership. Thaddeus Stevens died in August 1868, and his death brought joy to the hearts of conservative white Southerners. "The prayers of the righteous have at last removed the Congressional curse!" wrote one southern editor. "May his new iron-works wean him from earth and the fires of his new furnaces never go out!" Many of Stevens's Republican colleagues in the House sighed in relief, too, as they were freed from his stern parliamentary leadership; and so did the bankers and bondholders who distrusted this monetary heretic.

Stevens was only one of many radicals who were removed from public life by death or retirement. Joshua R. Giddings, Edwin M. Stanton, and Salmon P. Chase joined Stevens in the hell to which conservatives had consigned them; in 1869 Benjamin F. Wade lost his seat in the Senate, and the next year George W. Julian lost his seat in the House. Charles Sumner and Carl Schurz broke with Grant early in his first administration, and Grant's henchmen completely destroyed Sumner's power in the Senate. Horace Greeley, editor of the New York *Tribune*, and Edwin L. Godkin, editor of the *Nation*, both repudiated Grant and the Republican policy in the South. Many former abolitionists showed little understanding of the free Negro's postwar problems. In short, the force of a great movement for social reform seemed to be spent, and its leadership was being lost.

To replace the old Republican radicals a new set of leaders emerged and soon won a dominant position in the Grant administration. These new leaders were appropriately called stalwarts, for in conformance with the party's changed role they favored not radicalism, not reform, but the *status quo*. Some of the stalwarts were ruthless bosses of state political machines; some were almost paid retainers of railroad, oil, textile, and steel interests. They were the men who completed the institutionalization of the Republican party; who, more than ever before, made the quest for office an end in itself; and who, through the spoils system, prostituted the federal civil service. Among the more colorful of the stalwart leaders were several of the state bosses: Senator Oliver P. Morton of Indiana, Senator Roscoe Conkling of New York, Senator Simon Cameron of Pennsylvania, and Representative Benjamin F. Butler of Massachusetts.

The remnants of the old crusading radicals found this new Republican leadership appalling, and they began to wonder whether their party had outlived its usefulness. "Like all parties that have an undisturbed power for a long time," wrote Senator James W. Grimes of Iowa, the Republican party "has become corrupt, and I believe it is today the most corrupt and debauched political party that has ever existed." George W. Julian, one of the most dedicated radicals of the 1860's, revealed his disillusionment when, in 1884, he wrote his political recollections. To begin with, he recalled, the Republican movement had been "a political combination, rather than a party. Its action was inspired less by a creed than an object, and that object was to dedicate our National Territories to freedom, and to denationalize slavery. . . . The organization was created to deal with this single question, and would not have existed without it." By the 1870's many regarded the Republican party "as a spent political force, although it had received a momentum which threatened to outlast its mission." Julian then spoke of the "new problems" of the postwar years; and, significantly, he did not count the plight of the southern Negroes among them. He had turned his attention to other things: "Our tariff legislation called for a thorough revision. Our Civil Service was becoming a system of political prostitution. Roguery and plunder, born of the multiplied temptations which the war had furnished, had stealthily crept into the management of public affairs." But the Republican party, "led by base men," ignored all these issues and sought to retain its power "by artful appeals to the memories of the past." What the country needed, Julian concluded, "was not . . . the fostering of sectional hate, but oblivion of the past, and an earnest . . . endeavor to grapple with questions of practical administration."

It was sentiment such as this that caused many of the old reformers to repudiate Grant in 1872, to help form the so-called Liberal Republican party, and to support its candidate, Horace Greeley, for the presidency. Schurz, Julian, Sumner, Theodore Tilton, David Dudley Field, and many other one-time radicals were among the rebels in that campaign. Their platform was a plea for civil service reform and for honesty and efficiency in government. Though accepting the Fourteenth and Fifteenth Amendments, the platform also demanded universal amnesty and an end to military rule in the South. To these disenchanted men the radical governments had failed, the Negro as a freedman had been a disappointment,[3] and home rule under the old white leadership was the only way to restore honest government.

---

[3] Sumner and some of the old abolitionist leaders, however, did not lose faith in the Negro.

Ironically, it was the pro-Grant stalwart faction of the Republican party that continued to stand by the southern Negroes and to demand that their civil and political rights be protected. The stalwarts still hoped to maintain a southern Republican party with Negro votes; and as political realists who did not expect too much of frail humanity, they were not so easily disillusioned with the radical governments as were the moral reformers. Since the Grant Republicans won the election of 1872, the federal government stood by the carpetbaggers, scalawags, and Negroes a while longer. But the party split—the disaffection of the Liberal Republicans and their concentration on other issues—was a clear sign that the crusade for Negro rights had lost its vitality.

While factionalism troubled the national Republican organization, it soon began to undermine the southern radical governments as well. Sometimes party divisions resulted from the rivalry of political leaders, or from conflicts over the distribution of offices; sometimes they reflected the suspicions that carpetbaggers, scalawags, or Negroes often felt for one another; sometimes they were the product of struggles among rival business groups for legislative favors; and sometimes they were the consequence of reform movements within the radical organizations. In South Carolina, for example, after the corrupt scalawag governor, Franklin J. Moses, was replaced by the honest and conscientious carpetbagger, Daniel H. Chamberlain, a bitter feud developed between the Moses and Chamberlain factions. In Tennessee native Unionists, according to one report, considered the carpetbaggers to be "mere office hunting adventurers who come south with no intention of permanently residing here." In Mississippi the first radical governor, James L. Alcorn, a scalawag, tried to get control of the party for the local Whigs. But other Mississippi radicals resented this, and in 1873 they superseded Alcorn with the carpetbagger Adelbert Ames. As a result, Alcorn and his disappointed Whig followers soon drifted over to the Democrats. In Louisiana there was a violent struggle between the Henry C. Warmoth (anti-Grant) Republicans and the William P. Kellogg (pro-Grant) Republicans. In the state election of 1872 both factions claimed victory, but Grant gave his support to the Kellogg faction, a decision which the Warmoth faction contested for the next four years. Conflicts such as these dissipated Republican strength, and the Democrats exploited them to the utmost.

Meanwhile, southern Democrats gained strength when Congress finally removed the political disabilities from most of the prewar leadership. In May 1872, because of pressure from the Liberal Republicans, Congress passed a general amnesty act which restored the right of officeholding to the vast majority of those who had been disqualified under the provisions of the Fourteenth Amendment. After the passage of this act only a few hundred ex-Confederates remained unpardoned. Those not included in the amnesty of 1872 were, according to the act, Confederates who had been "Senators and Representatives of the thirty-sixth and thirty-seventh Congresses [1859–63], officers in the judicial, military, and naval service of the United States, heads of departments, and foreign ministers of the United States." The last of these, incidentally, did not receive their pardons until the time of the Spanish-American War.

As the Republican party was being weakened by factionalism and the Democratic party strengthened by the recovery of its old southern leadership, radical reconstruction continued to be threatened by another force of undiminished power: race prejudice. This was a serious problem in the North as well as in the South, because only a minority of Northerners felt any genuine enthusiasm for the radical program of equal civil and political rights for both races. Many of the reformers, as we have seen, lost faith in, or patience with, the southern Negroes; while everywhere in the North the notion of the Negro's innate racial inferiority remained almost unchallenged. Even a federal officer who had worked with the Negroes and sympathized with those who would help them was pessimistic about their prospects. "It is a moot point," he wrote, "whether colored children are as quick at learning as white children. I should say not; certainly those I saw could not compare with the Caucasian youngster of ten or twelve . . .; they were inferior to him, not only in knowledge, but in the facility of acquisition. . . . I am convinced that the Negro as he is, no matter how educated, is not the mental equal of the European."

But it was the ravings of northern Democratic politicians, who inflamed the prejudices of white men in every political campaign, that caused so many Northerners to fear the consequences of the radical program. Senator Thomas A. Hendricks of Indiana, Democratic minority leader, provided a typical example in the following remarks: "I say that we are not of the same race; we are so different that we ought not to compose one political community. . . . I say . . . this is a white man's Government, made by the white man for the white man. . . . I am not in favor of giving the colored man a vote, because I think we should remain a political community of white people. I do not think it is for the good of either race that we should attempt to make the Government a mixed Government of white and black. . . . I am not in favor of attempting to mix these races. I want to see the white race kept a white race, and the power in this country without mixture and without an attempt at mixture." Democrats combined ominous predictions of racial amalgamation such as this with warnings to white workingmen that Republicans hoped to flood northern industrial cities with cheap Negro labor.

In 1870, the *Atlantic Monthly,* a favorite periodical of northern intellectuals, published some allegedly informed observations about the Negro by an ex-Southerner, Nathaniel S. Shaler, who had served in the Union army. Conditions among the Negroes, Shaler wrote, had not changed as much as was often supposed. Being "naturally docile," they were not self-assertive unless instigated by "dangerous friends belonging to the other race." Their general demeanor was much as it had been when they were slaves, except that they were "perhaps less merry than before; the careless laugh of the old slave is now rarely heard, for it belonged to a creature who had never pondered the question of where his next meal was to come from." Unless one understood "how thoroughly exotic the Negro is," Shaler added, "one cannot appreciate the difficulties of making him a part of the social system which fits us. . . . Under his covering of imitated manners . . . slumber the passions of a mental organization widely differing from our own. . . . The school has its place in civilization . . . but it is the last step in the development of a race, not the first, and its value consists in the fact that it is the final result of the education of a thousand years of effort; and when we undertake to civilize a race as foreign to us in every trait as the negroes, by imposing on them this final product of our national growth, we wrong ourselves and them." Northerners were thus already being given a sentimentalized version of slavery; and they were being told, in effect, that only Southerners understood the Negro and that formal education for the Negro was futile.

In the South the fact that the radical governments were committed to equal civil rights for the two races and were supported by Negro votes was enough to arouse most white farmers and mechanics to vigorous opposition. They opposed the radical program for the same reason that they had supported slavery. As men of low status and low income they were keenly aware that the Negroes were potential social and economic competitors. For lower-class whites the most readily available means of achieving personal prestige was a caste system designed to keep the Negro "in his place" and to give them a superior and privileged position as members of the white race. In the politics of this caste-ridden society the conservative Democratic party gained the advantage of being identified with the "better people," above all, of being known as "the white man's party."

The notion that Negroes belonged to an inferior race bolstered the belief that their subordination to the whites was natural and inevitable. But the psychological needs of the average lower-class white were even more important; indeed, they made the question of the Negro's innate capacities more or less irrelevant. For the low-status white man the essential fact of life was the color of his skin. "I may be poor and my manners may be crude," he told the world, "but I am a white man. And because I am a white man, I have the right to be treated with respect by Negroes. That I am poor is not as important as that I am a *white* man; and no Negro is ever going to forget that he is *not* a white man."

On the other hand, the reaction of upper-class Southerners to the race policies of the radicals was in many cases quite different. They, too, believed in white supremacy, but they seldom made the crusade to keep the Negroes a subordinate caste the central purpose of their lives. They did not look upon Negroes as economic competitors but as an essential labor supply; their secure social position made them less reluctant to grant Negroes equal civil and political rights. In fact, a very considerable proportion of the large property holders, perhaps a majority, during the years of reconstruction eventually came around to accepting Negro suffrage and the legal equality of the two races. Given the removal of federal troops, they were confident that they would be able to control a large part of the Negro vote; they would find co-operative Negro leaders who would support them as the defenders of the Negroes against the hostile lower-class whites. Wade Hampton, an aristocratic South Carolinian, argued that the only remaining hope was to "direct the Negro vote. . . . Now how shall we do this? Simply by making the Negro a Southern man, and if you will, a Democrat, anything but a Radical."

Thus in the politics of the reconstruction era the appeal of conservative Democrats was sometimes a little contradictory. Some politicians, taking the position of upper-class property holders, accepted Negro suffrage and tried to manipulate the Negro vote in favor of the Democrats. When, in 1876, Wade Hampton ran for governor of South Carolina, he told the Negroes: "We want your votes; we don't want you to be deprived of them. . . . I pledge my faith, and I pledge it for those gentlemen who are in the ticket with me, that if we are elected, as far as in us lies, *we will observe, protect, and defend the rights of the colored man as quickly as any man in South Carolina.*"

Most Democratic politicians, however, resorted to race demagoguery; and even those who spoke to the Negroes as Hampton did would often exploit the race issue when bidding for the votes of lower-class whites. They raised the banner of white supremacy and used it as effectively as the radicals in the North used the bloody shirt. They organized "White Men's Clubs," while their newspapers and orators made incendiary appeals to race bigotry. They de-

scribed the uncontrolled Negro male as a perpetual men-
ace to southern white womanhood; they predicted that the
radicals would produce in the South a "mongrel" race. To
prevent the "Africanization" of the South, they demanded:
"A white man in a white man's place. A black man in a
black man's place. Each according to the eternal fitness of
things." An appeal of South Carolina Democrats on behalf
of "the proud Caucasian race, whose sovereignty on earth
God has ordained" protested against the "subversion of
the great social law, whereby an ignorant and depraved
race is placed in power and influence above the virtuous,
the educated and the refined." The "leading ideas" of
Mississippi Democrats, according to a blunt local editor,
were "that white men shall govern, that niggers are not
rightly entitled to vote, and that . . . niggers will be placed
upon the same footing with white minors who do not vote
or hold office." Democrats combined appeals such as these
with intense social pressure on white men who collaborated with Negroes in radical politics. Newspapers published the names of the white renegades, and they were
socially ostracized. "They don't associate with my family,
or the families of republicans," wrote a Mississippi physi-
cian who was a scalawag. "We have to make what little association we have with ourselves."

This kind of pressure not only prevented the scalawag
ranks from growing but caused them to shrink. In the later
years of reconstruction, white Southerners deserted the
radicals by the thousands, so that in the South the Republican party became increasingly a party of Negroes and
carpetbaggers. When Henry Lusk, a prominent Mississippi
scalawag, announced that he was quitting the Republicans, he explained his reasons to a Negro friend: "No
white man can live in the South in the future and act with
any other than the Democratic party unless he is willing

and prepared to live a life of social isolation and remain in political oblivion. . . . I have two grown sons. There is, no doubt . . . a brilliant and successful future before them if they are Democrats; otherwise, not. . . . My daughters are the pride of my home. I cannot afford to have them suffer the humiliating consequences of the social ostracism to which they may be subjected if I remain in the Republican party. . . . I must yield to the inevitable and surrender my convictions upon the altar of my family's good."

At least as important a factor as racial demagoguery in the overthrow of the radical regimes was the resort to physical violence. Many years later, Adelbert Ames, Mississippi's last radical governor, recalled how the whites rationalized their illegal acts. As they saw it, an "unjust and tyrannical power . . . had filled their state with mourning, beggared them, freed their slaves and as a last insult and injury made the ex-slave a political equal. They resisted by intimidation, violence and murder."[4]

Organized terrorism was popularly associated with the Ku Klux Klan, formed in Tennessee in 1866, but the Klan was only one of many such organizations, which included the Knights of the White Camelia, the White Brotherhood, the Pale Faces, and the '76 Association. These societies drew their membership chiefly, but by no means exclusively, from the poor whites and yeoman farmers, who apparently found their rituals and organizational terminology, as well as their purposes, irresistible. The local Klan units were called dens; these were organized into provinces, the provinces into dominions, the dominions into realms, and the whole into an empire, "The Invisible Empire of the South." At the head was a grand wizard and ten genii; subordinate to them were grand dragons, furies, hydras, titans, and night-hawks.

---

[4] Quoted in Wharton, *The Negro in Mississippi*, p. 197.

Members of the dens were called ghouls, and the den master was a cyclops. "This is an institution of Chivalry, Humanity, Mercy, and Patriotism," declared the Klan's prescript, "embodying in its genius and its principles all that is chivalric in conduct, noble in sentiment, generous in manhood, and patriotic in purpose." Its purposes were, among others, to "protect the weak, the innocent, and the defenseless" and to "protect and defend the Constitution of the United States." Presumably in pursuit of these goals candidates for membership had to affirm that they were "opposed to negro equality, both social and political," and "in favor of a white man's government."

The Klansmen dressed in white robes and hoods and rode white sheeted horses to spread terror among the radicals, Negro and white. They broke up Republican meetings, threatened radical leaders, whipped Negro militiamen, and drove Negroes away from the polls. They were guilty of shootings, murders, and plundering, until their lawlessness caused Klan leaders themselves to try, unsuccessfully, to disband the organization. Eventually Congress conducted an elaborate investigation and adopted legislation designed to suppress organized terrorism. Two so-called Force Acts, passed on May 31, 1870, and February 28, 1871, provided that the use of force or intimidation to prevent citizens from voting was to be punished by fine or imprisonment, authorized the President to use the military when necessary to enforce the Fifteenth Amendment, and placed congressional elections under federal supervision. A third Force Act, the Ku Klux Act of April 20, 1871, imposed heavier penalties on persons who "shall conspire together, or go in disguise . . . for the purpose . . . of depriving any person or any class of persons of the equal protection of the laws, or of equal privileges or immunities under the laws." Additional federal troops were sent into the South, and President Grant suspended the writ of habeas corpus in a number of South Carolina counties. After scores of arrests, fines, and imprisonments, the Klan's power was finally broken, and by 1872 it had almost disappeared.

But the end of the Klan was not the end of organized violence, for violence was a basic part of the crusade against the radicals in every southern state. The Klan had done this rugged work in Virginia, North Carolina, Tennessee, and Georgia, where the conservatives had regained control between 1869 and 1871; but similar groups arose in the seven remaining southern states. The pattern of violence that conservatives developed in Mississippi, generally known as the Mississippi Plan, sometimes as the "shotgun policy," was typical. In the state election of 1875, Mississippi Democrats simply resolved to use as much force as was necessary in order to win.[5] During the campaign a local newspaper announced this purpose with complete candor: "All other means having been exhausted to abate the horrible condition of things, the thieves and robbers, and scoundrels, white and black, deserve death and ought to be killed. . . . [They] ought to be compelled to leave the state or abide the consequences. . . . Carry the election peaceably if we can, forcibly if we must." According to another editor: "The present contest is rather a revolution than a political campaign—it is the rebellion, if you see fit to apply that term, of a down-trodden people against an absolutism imposed by their own hirelings . . ."

To implement the Mississippi Plan local Democratic clubs organized themselves into irregular militia companies and armed themselves with rifles. They drilled and

---

[5] For a full account of the Mississippi election of 1875 see Wharton, *The Negro in Mississippi*, pp. 181–98. The account presented here summarizes Wharton's findings.

paraded through the areas of heavy Negro population; they enrolled Negro leaders in so-called "dead-books"; they dispersed Republican meetings; they forced Negroes at rifle point to listen to Democratic speakers; they deliberately provoked riots in which hundreds of Negroes were killed; and they posted armed pickets at registration places to prevent Negroes from registering. Before long, in many Mississippi counties, the Republicans simply abandoned any attempt to hold political meetings.

In the face of this violence radical Governor Ames was completely helpless. In September 1875, he issued a proclamation ordering all private militia companies to disperse, but the Democrats treated his proclamation as a joke. Ames then considered forming a regular state militia, but he would have been unable to get any but Negroes to serve, and this would have led to a disastrous race war. So he gave up the idea; in fact, he gave up entirely. Ames concluded that there was no way to prevent the Democrats from carrying the election, and his chief concern was to find some way to stop the killing of Negroes.

On election day thousands of terrified Negroes were hiding in the swamps or staying in their cabins. In some places the only Negroes who could vote were those who showed Democratic ballots or who were accompanied to the polls by white men. Many who were bold enough to carry Republican ballots were fired upon or driven away from the polls. Vernon Wharton describes what happened at Aberdeen when a body of Negroes approached the polls: "E. O. Sykes, in charge of the Democratic war department, posted the cavalry he had imported from Alabama, surrounded the Negroes with infantry, loaded a cannon with chains and slugs, and then sent a strong-arm squad into the crowd to beat the Negroes over the head. . . . The Republican sheriff, an ex-Confederate, locked himself in his own jail." The Democrats of Aberdeen thus achieved a majority of 1,175, whereas in 1871 the Republicans had a majority of 648. In three Mississippi counties, Tishomingo, Yazoo, and Kemper, the Republicans polled twelve, seven, and four votes respectively. And so the Democrats won, and Mississippi was "redeemed."

This, essentially, was the pattern of violence in the remaining southern states. In South Carolina, in 1876, the Rifle Clubs and Wade Hampton's Red Shirts executed the Mississippi Plan. "'They intend to carry this election," wrote a reporter for the Cincinnati *Commercial*. "The programme [is] to have 'rifle clubs' all over the State, and, while avoiding actual bloodshed as much as possible, to so impress the blacks that they, or a number of them, will feel impelled to vote with the whites out of actual fear." Early in July a serious race riot in Hamburg was the prelude to what Governor Chamberlain described as "a campaign of blood and violence . . . [one that] is popularly known as a campaign conducted on the 'Mississippi plan.' " The historian of reconstruction in Florida, though dealing with the subject of violence with a certain delicacy, makes clear enough what happened in that state. "The election methods of Conservative reformers in 1876," he writes, "when judged apart from environment and in the light of exalted ethics, were rather bad. Democrats . . . bulldozed opponents at the end of a halter or the point of a gun into voting with them or not voting at all." The white Southerner "resorted to physical violence . . . in one of the most sinister and interesting contests of modern times. And in this contest for a very necessary supremacy many a foul crime was committed by white against black. . . . The negro was first freed, then enfranchised, then launched into practical politics, and then mercilessly beaten into reasonable subjection."[6]

The conservatives, however, often resorted to forms of

---

[6] Davis, *Civil War and Reconstruction in Florida*, pp. 585–6, 703–4.

intimidation more subtle than overt terrorism. They found that often a mere threat of violence was sufficient to keep Republicans away from the polls. Economic coercion was particularly effective when used against the Negroes. A Henry County, Alabama, landlord required two Negro laborers to sign the following contract before giving them employment: "That said Laborers shall not attach themselves, belong to or in any way perform any of the obligations required of what is known as the 'Loyal League Society' or attend elections or political meetings without the consent of the employer." White landowners made agreements not to employ or give assistance to Negroes who voted Republican. Observers were placed at the polls, and after each election the names of those not to be employed were printed in the newspapers. In Alabama, complained a scalawag, the "oligarchy in the rebel ranks . . . held the bread-basket before the hungry gaze of the voters, both white and colored . . . and said to hundreds and thousands of them vote if you dare and the earth be your bed and the stones be your bread." During the state campaign of 1875 a Mississippi editor advised conservatives "to use the great and all-powerful weapon that is in our control; we should not falter in the pledge to ourselves and our neighbors to discharge from our employ and our friendship forever, every laborer who persists in the diabolical war that has been waged against the white man and his interests ever since the negro has been a voter."

These were the various forces operating against the radicals within the South. But if violence and intimidation were the weapons of the conservatives, why was there no effective federal intervention? Why did President Grant and Congress permit the Mississippi Plan to succeed? Why were the Fourteenth and Fifteenth Amendments, the Force Acts, and the Civil Rights Acts not enforced? Why were more federal troops not sent into the South to protect the Negroes? In answering these questions some additional reasons for the collapse of the radical governments may be discovered.

In the first place, it should be obvious that once the Republicans rejected land reform and abolished the Freedmen's Bureau, their political alliance with southern Negroes was at best an uneasy one. Negroes joined the Republican party because it had given them civil and political rights and because southern white Democrats were hostile to them, not because they found Republican policies on other postwar issues particularly attractive. As small farmers, tenants, sharecroppers, and unskilled rural and urban laborers, their interests were far removed from those of the leaders of northern business enterprise to whom most Republican legislators usually deferred on matters of economic policy. Here and there Negro farm laborers tried to organize, and occasionally they attempted through strikes and collective bargaining to achieve a minimum wage. In the early 1870's, when the Granger movement spread into the South, Negroes began to organize their own Granges and to discuss the plight of the American farmer. Such activities were well calculated to cool the ardor of stalwart Republicans for the Negroes as political allies. In 1871 a northern Republican, observing that in Georgia some six thousand adult whites were illiterate, warned that "if to them were added the whole bulk of the Negro population, so vast a mass of ignorance would be found that, if combined for any political purpose it would sweep away all opposition the intelligent class might make. Many thoughtful men are apprehensive that the ignorant voters will, in the future, form a party by themselves as dangerous to the interests of society as the communists of France."

Meanwhile, at the time that the Liberal Republicans were denouncing their party's southern policy, a number of regular Republicans began to toy with Lincoln's scheme of appealing to the Whiggish propertied elements in the South. Jacob D. Cox of Ohio, Grant's first Secretary of the Interior, was one of the earliest to advocate such a course. Never enthusiastic about radical reconstruction, Cox had described it privately as "one of those revolutionary excesses which play most powerfully into an adversary's hands." In 1871 he suggested, again privately, that the Republican party ought to make peace with, and bid for the support of, the "thinking and influential native southerners," the "intelligent, well-to-do, and controlling class." The following year a Virginia conservative told Schurz that many white Southerners "take the Democratic party as the choice of evils. Many who now vote with the Radicals, a large number of old Whigs, and all who call themselves conservatives . . . want to defeat both Radicalism and Democracy." Even some of the carpetbaggers broke with the Negroes and became "independent" Republicans in alliance with conservative southern whites. These were the seeds from which eventually grew the Compromise of 1877 and the subsequent Republican abandonment of the Negro.

Northern businessmen, who became increasingly concerned about continued turbulence in the South, were especially eager to have the Republican party come to terms with conservative Southerners. Capitalists with an interest in the South as a field for investment had at first given their support to the Johnson program; but they were soon disillusioned with the President and turned to the radicals. What businessmen sought were conditions favorable to northern economic penetration of the South, and the radicals aided them, especially the railroad promoters, in a number of ways. However, they were distressed by the violence and, in some cases, financial instability that were a part of southern politics during the radical regimes; for these conditions were bad for trade and frightened capital away.

By 1870 the New York *Commercial and Financial Chronicle*, the New York *Tribune*, and the *Nation* were demanding an end to radical reconstruction, because it was paralyzing southern business and discouraging those who had capital to invest in that section. In May the *Nation* reported that "businessmen of the highest character" from New York and Boston had been examining conditions in the South "with reference to investments" and that they had found the state of affairs quite discouraging. Five years later, William E. Dodge, a New York capitalist and Grant Republican, returned to the same theme. "What the South now needs," he said, "is capital to develop her resources, but this she cannot obtain till confidence in her state governments can be restored, and this will never be done by federal bayonets. . . . As merchants we want to see the South gain her normal condition in the commerce of the country; nor can we hope for a general revival of business while things remain as they are." As for the southern Negroes, Dodge concluded that it had been a mistake to make them feel "that the United States government was their special friend, rather than those with whom their lot is cast, among whom they must live and for whom they must work. We have tried this long enough. Now let the South alone."

Thus Republican politicians found less and less sympathy among northern businessmen for their southern program. It appeared that only southern conservatives could restore order and political stability and thus create conditions favorable to economic development with northern capital. Moreover, since southern conservatives were being converted to the gospel of a "New South" which would emphasize commerce and industry, they could now be relied upon to give northern businessmen a friendly welcome. Radical reconstruction was then not only not essential, it was a nuisance.

Republican politicians also found that Northerners in general were growing tired of the reconstruction issue, that appeals to them on behalf of southern Negroes were greeted with massive indifference. Waving the bloody shirt to revive the passions of the Civil War eventually reached the point of diminishing returns; for, by the 1870's, most Northerners were as little concerned about the alleged disloyalty of southern white men as they were about reports of continued outrages against southern Negroes.

Then came the business panic of 1873, followed by four years of severe depression and the exposure of scandals in the Grant administration. These events dealt the American people a series of shattering blows. Grant, once the great military hero and the embodiment of numerous national virtues, though personally honest, was now associated with corruption and the debasement of the civil service. Jay Cooke, the most powerful banker in America, presumed to be a model of business probity, went bankrupt because he speculated recklessly in railroad securities. Even the Reverend Henry Ward Beecher of Plymouth Church in Brooklyn, the best-known preacher in America, to whom many middle-class Protestants looked for moral guidance, became involved at this inopportune time in a private scandal that culminated in a trial for adultery. If men such as Grant, Cooke, and Beecher, Republicans all, had feet of clay, the country was in a sorry state. To the *Nation* the remedy was clear: give the South home rule, and the country would "once more resume the path of careful and orderly progress from which the slavery agitation and its consequences have during the last generation driven us. It were better that all the blacks and whites now living south of Mason and Dixon's line were sunk in the sea than go on as we are going now, for we are forming habits and establishing precedents which can only lead to a result over which many generations would mourn and wonder."

As they became concerned about business stagnation, unemployment, collapsing farm prices, and the decay of public and private morals, Northerners not only lost interest in reconstruction but temporarily lost faith in the Republican party. The bloody shirt could no longer control the outcome of an election, and in 1874 the Republicans lost control of the House of Representatives—their first political defeat in a national election since the Civil War. After the Democrats gained a majority in the House, there was no chance that additional federal protection would be given to southern Negroes. Instead, the House Democrats, in 1876, refused to pass an army appropriation bill in order to force the President to withdraw federal troops from the South. It was then that one Republican politician concluded that the people were bored with the "worn-out cry of 'southern outrages' "; another now remembered that the Civil War had not been fought primarily to free the slaves—that the Negro was not "the end and aim of all our effort."

Under these circumstances the absence of federal intervention when the Mississippi Plan went into operation is understandable. In 1875, Governor Ames begged Grant's Attorney General, Edwards Pierrepont, to give protection to the Negroes of his state during that violent election. But the federal government took no action. A delegation of Republicans from Ohio, where an election was also be-

The Era of Reconstruction

ing held that year, warned President Grant that if he sent
troops to Mississippi his party would lose Ohio. Grant decided to save Ohio and sacrifice the Negroes of Mississippi.
His Attorney General's reply to Governor Ames was that
the people were "tired of these annual autumnal out-
breaks in the South." With this "flippant utterance," Ames
later recalled, "the executive branch of the National government announced that it had decided that the reconstruction acts of congress were a failure."[7]

During the state and presidential elections of 1876,
when violence broke out in South Carolina, Florida, and
Louisiana, President Grant would do nothing more than
issue a sanctimonious proclamation. Indeed, when the outcome of that election was in dispute, Republicans had to
bargain hard with southern Democrats in order to secure
the peaceful inauguration of Rutherford B. Hayes. In one
last sectional compromise, that of 1877, the Republicans
promised to remove the remaining federal troops in the
South, to be fair to Southerners in the distribution of federal patronage, and to vote funds for a number of southern internal improvements. In return, southern Democrats
agreed to acquiesce in the inauguration of Hayes and to
deal fairly with the Negroes.

The Compromise of 1877 signified the final end of radical reconstruction, for with the removal of federal troops,
the last of the radical regimes collapsed. Soon after his inauguration President Hayes made a goodwill tour of the
South. Conservative Democratic leaders, such as Governor
Wade Hampton of South Carolina, greeted him cordially
and assured him that peace and racial harmony now
reigned in the South. Hayes tried hard to believe it, because he hoped so much that it was true.

"What is the President's Southern policy?" asked ex-

---

[7] Quoted in Wharton, *The Negro in Mississippi*, p. 194.

VII: *Triumph of the Conservatives*

Governor Chamberlain of South Carolina. Judged by its results, "it consists in the abandonment of Southern Republicans, and especially the colored race, to the control and rule not only of the Democratic party, but of that class at the South which regarded slavery as a Divine Institution, which waged four years of destructive war for its perpetuation, which steadily opposed citizenship and suffrage for the negro—in a word, a class whose traditions, principles, and history are opposed to every step and feature of what Republicans call our national progress since 1860."

It was in the 1870's, then, and not in 1865, that the idealism of the antislavery crusade finally died. Along with the loss of the idealism that had been one of the prime motivating forces behind radical reconstruction, the practical considerations also lost their relevance. Whereas in 1865 the urban middle classes still regarded the agrarian South and West as a serious threat, by the 1870's their position was consolidated and their power supreme. By then the leaders of business enterprise had so far penetrated the Democratic party and had so much influence among the so-called "redeemers" of the South that they no longer equated Republican political defeat with economic disaster. Samuel J. Tilden, the Democratic presidential candidate in 1876, was a wealthy, conservative New York corporation lawyer, thoroughly "sound" on monetary, banking, and fiscal policy, in no respect unfriendly to business interests. Whichever way the presidential election of 1876 had gone, these interests could hardly have lost. Grover Cleveland, the only Democrat elected President between James Buchanan before the Civil War and Woodrow Wilson in the twentieth century, was also "sound" and conservative on all the economic issues of his day.

As for the Republican party, it too felt more secure than

it had before. In 1865 it was still uncertain whether this party, born of crisis, could survive in a reunited, peaceful Union in which the slavery issue was resolved. But by the 1870's the party was firmly established, had an efficient, powerful, amply endowed organization, and had the unswerving support of a mass of loyal voters. True, the Republicans lost the congressional elections of 1874 and almost lost the presidency in 1876, but this could be attributed to the depression and abnormal conditions. Normally, in order to exist as a major national party, Republicans no longer needed the votes of southern Negroes. The reason for this was that during and since the war they had won control of the Old Northwest, once a stronghold of agrarianism and copperheadism.[8] Indeed, a significant chapter in the history of reconstruction is the political and economic reconstruction of this flourishing region. The Civil War, the identification of the Republican party with nationalism and patriotism, the veteran vote, the Homestead Act, and federal appropriations for internal improvements all helped to make the states of the Old Northwest Republican strongholds. Moreover, the westward advance of the industrial revolution—the growth of urban centers such as Cleveland, Detroit, and Chicago —identified powerful economic groups in the Old Northwest with the industrial interests of the Northeast.

How these western states voted in the eleven presidential elections between 1868 and 1908 is significant when it is remembered that they had consistently gone Democratic before the Civil War. In eight elections the Old Northwest went Republican unanimously. Of the seven states in this region, Indiana voted Democratic three times, Illinois and Wisconsin once, the rest never. Thus,

---

[8] The states of the Old Northwest include Ohio, Indiana, Illinois, Michigan, Wisconsin, Minnesota, and Iowa.

with the Old Northwest made safe for the Republican party, the political motive for radical reconstruction vanished, and practical Republicans could afford to abandon the southern Negro. With the decline of the idealism and the disappearance of the realistic political and economic considerations that had supported it, radical reconstruction came to an end.

Viewing radical reconstruction with its three chief motivating forces in mind, are we to call it a success or a failure? Insofar as its purpose was to consolidate the position of American industrial capitalism, it was doubtless a striking success. During the last three decades of the nineteenth century, social and economic reformers subjected irresponsible business entrepreneurs to constant attack, but they won no significant victories. In fact, they met constant defeat, climaxed by the failure of the Populists in the 1890's. With William McKinley, the conservative son of an Ohio industrialist, installed in power in 1897, American capitalism rode to the end of the nineteenth century with its power uncurbed and its supremacy not yet effectively challenged. Above all, the conservative Democratic leaders of the New South were no longer enemies but allies.

Politically, radical reconstruction was also a success. Even though Republicans failed in their effort to establish an effective and durable organization in the South, they nevertheless emerged from the era of reconstruction in a powerful position. Most of their subsequent political victories were narrow; sometimes they lost a congressional campaign. But until Wilson's election in 1912, only once, in 1892, did the Democrats win control of the presidency and both houses of Congress simultaneously. And if conservative Republican Congressmen counted almost no

Southerners in their caucus, they found a large number of southern Democrats remarkably easy to work with. The coalition of northern Republicans and southern Dixie-crats, so powerful in recent Congresses, was an important fact of American political life as early as the 1880's. The coalition had to be an informal one and had to endure a great deal of partisan rhetoric, but it was real nonetheless.

Finally, we come to the idealistic aim of the radicals to make southern society more democratic, especially to make the emancipation of the Negroes something more than an empty gesture. In the short run this was their greatest fail-ure. In the rural South the basic socioeconomic pattern was not destroyed, for share-cropping replaced the ante-bellum slave-plantation system. Most of the upper-class large landowners survived the ordeal of war and recon-struction, and the mass of Negroes remained a dependent, propertyless peasantry. After reconstruction, in spite of the Fourteenth and Fifteenth Amendments, the Negroes were denied equal civil and political rights. In 1883 the Supreme Court invalidated the Civil Rights Act of 1875; in 1894 Congress repealed the Force Acts; and in 1896 the Supreme Court sanctioned social segregation if Ne-groes were provided "equal" accommodations. Thus Ne-groes were denied federal protection, and by the end of the nineteenth century the Republican party had nearly forgotten them. In place of slavery a caste system reduced Negroes to an inferior type of citizenship; social segrega-tion gave them inferior educational and recreational facil-ities; and a pattern of so-called "race etiquette" forced them to pay deference to all white men. Negroes, in short, were only half emancipated.

Still, no one could quite forget that the Fourteenth and Fifteenth Amendments were now part of the federal Con-stitution. As a result, Negroes could no longer be deprived of the right to vote, except by extralegal coercion or by some devious subterfuge. They could not be deprived of equal civil rights, except by deceit. They could not be segregated in public places, except by the spurious argument that this did not in fact deprive them of the equal protection of the laws. Thus Negroes were no longer denied equality by the plain language of the law, as they had been before radical reconstruction, but only by coercion, by subterfuge, by deceit, and by spurious legalisms. For a time, of course, the denial of equality was as effective one way as the other; but when it was sanctioned by the laws of the Johnson governments and approved by the federal government, there was no hope. When, however, state-imposed discrimination was, in effect, an evasion of the supreme law of the land, the odds, in the long run, were on the side of the Negro.

The Fourteenth and Fifteenth Amendments, which could have been adopted only under the conditions of radical reconstruction, make the blunders of that era, tragic though they were, dwindle into insignificance. For if it was worth four years of civil war to save the Union, it was worth a few years of radical reconstruction to give the American Negro the ultimate promise of equal civil and political rights.

Bibliographical Note

This bibliographical note is not an exhaustive compilation of reconstruction literature or of the books and articles that I have consulted. Rather, it is highly selective, containing only those items that I have drawn on for factual material, that have influenced my interpretations, or that represent significant points of view in reconstruction historiography. For a comprehensive critical bibliography and a list of relevant biographies, autobiographies, memoirs, and published diaries and letters, see James G. Randall and David Donald, *The Civil War and Reconstruction* (Boston, 1961). The best recent historiographical essay is Bernard Weisberger, "The Dark and Bloody Ground of Reconstruction Historiography," *Journal of Southern History*, XXV (1959), pp. 427–47.

The following general works illustrate the traditional anti-radical interpretation of reconstruction: James Ford Rhodes, *History of the United States from the Compromise of 1850 . . .*, 7 vols. (New York, 1893–1906), Vols. V–VII; John W. Burgess, *Reconstruction and the Constitution, 1866–1876* (New York, 1902); William A. Dunning, *Reconstruction, Political and Economic, 1865–1877* (New York, 1907); Walter L. Fleming, *The Sequel of Appomattox* (New Haven, 1919); Claude G. Bowers, *The Tragic*

Era (Boston, 1929); James G. Randall, *The Civil War and Reconstruction* (Boston, 1937); Robert S. Henry, *The Story of Reconstruction* (Indianapolis, 1938); E. Merton Coulter, *The South during Reconstruction, 1865–1877* (Baton Rouge, 1947); and Hodding Carter, *The Angry Scar* (New York, 1959).

Much of the early protest against the anti-Negro, anti-radical biases of Rhodes and Dunning came from Negro and Marxist writers. A Negro historian, William E. B. Du Bois, in "Reconstruction and Its Benefits," *American Historical Review*, XV (1910), pp. 781–99, and an able Mississippi Negro politician, John R. Lynch, in *The Facts of Reconstruction* (New York, 1913), stress the positive achievements of the era. However, Du Bois's attempt at a full-scale revisionist study, *Black Reconstruction* (New York, 1935), is disappointing. Though rich in empirical data, the book presents a Marxian interpretation of southern reconstruction as a proletarian movement that is at best naïve. The Marxist historian James S. Allen, in *Reconstruction: The Battle for Democracy, 1865–1876* (New York, 1937) offers an interpretation that is more credible but equally schematic.

Recent non-Marxian revisionism began with a series of historiographical critiques of traditional interpretations. The most important of these is Howard K. Beale, "On Rewriting Reconstruction History," *American Historical Review*, XLV (1940), pp. 807–27. See also Alrutheus A. Taylor, "Historians of Reconstruction," *Journal of Negro History*, XXIII (1938), pp. 16–34; Francis B. Simkins, "New Viewpoints of Southern Reconstruction," *Journal of Southern History*, V (1939), pp. 49–61; T. Harry Williams, "An Analysis of Some Reconstruction Attitudes," *Journal of Southern History*, XII (1946), pp. 469–86; and John Hope Franklin, "Whither Reconstruction Historiography?" *Journal of Negro Education*, XVII (1948), pp. 446–61.

Most of the books and articles written by revisionists deal with some special aspect of reconstruction, but two syntheses are available: John Hope Franklin, *Reconstruction after the Civil War* (Chicago, 1961), and Randall and Donald, *Civil War and Reconstruction,* cited above. A comparison of the 1937 edition of Randall's book with Donald's 1961 revision will illustrate the points at which revisionists have modified the traditional interpretation of reconstruction. Revisionist interpretations are also incorporated in two valuable essays: Grady McWhiney, "Reconstruction: Index of Americanism," in Charles G. Sellers, Jr., ed., *The Southerner as American* (Chapel Hill, 1960), pp. 89–103; and C. Vann Woodward, "The Political Legacy of Reconstruction," in *The Burden of Southern History* (Baton Rouge, 1960), pp. 89–107.

Though the Lincoln literature is vast, there is no really satisfactory book-length study of his role in the reconstruction of the South. But there is an excellent essay on the subject in Richard N. Current, *The Lincoln Nobody Knows* (New York, 1958), pp. 237–65, and I have incorporated many of its ideas in my chapter on Lincoln. The following studies are useful: Charles H. McCarthy, *Lincoln's Plan of Reconstruction* (New York, 1901); James G. Randall, *Lincoln and the South* (Baton Rouge, 1946); and William B. Hesseltine, *Lincoln's Plan of Reconstruction* (Tuscaloosa, Ala., 1960). Of the many Lincoln biographies, the one most valuable for reconstruction is James G. Randall, *Lincoln the President,* 4 vols. (New York, 1945–55), Vol. IV, subtitled *Last Full Measure,* by Randall and Richard N. Current. See also James G. Randall, *Constitutional Problems under Lincoln* (Rev. ed., Chicago, 1951); Jonathan T. Dorris, *Pardon and Amnesty under Lincoln and Johnson* (Chapel Hill, 1953); David Donald, "The Radicals and Lincoln," in *Lincoln Reconsidered* (New York, 1956), pp. 103–27; and Benjamin Quarles, *Lincoln and the Negro* (New York, 1962).

Except for Rhodes and Burgess, who are critical, Andrew Johnson fares very well in the traditional reconstruction literature. He is also warmly defended by his four twentieth-century biographers: Robert W. Winston, *Andrew Johnson: Plebeian and Patriot* (New York, 1928); Lloyd P. Stryker, *Andrew Johnson: A Study in Courage* (New York, 1929); George Fort Milton, *The Age of Hate: Andrew Johnson and the Radicals* (New York, 1930); and Milton Lomask, *Andrew Johnson: President on Trial* (New York, 1960). Howard K. Beale, *The Critical Year: A Study of Andrew Johnson and Reconstruction* (New York, 1930), is another spirited defense of the President.

Three recent revisionist studies of exceptional importance are severely critical of Johnson's reconstruction policies and executive leadership. Eric L. McKitrick, *Andrew Johnson and Reconstruction* (Chicago, 1960), while showing little sympathy for the radicals, finds in Johnson's personal shortcomings and tactical blunders a fundamental cause for the failure to reconcile North and South and for the disruption of the nation's political life. LaWanda and John H. Cox, *Politics, Principle, and Prejudice, 1865–1866* (New York, 1963), holds Johnson responsible for initiating hostilities with Congress and for trying to isolate the radicals politically. W. R. Brock, *An American Crisis: Congress and Reconstruction, 1865–1867* (New York, 1963), finds Johnson inept, ignorant of northern public opinion, and out of contact with political reality.

Most of the traditional accounts of reconstruction describe the radicals as vindictive men or political opportunists. In the 1920's and 1930's, however, they were often described as the allies of northern business interests. See, for example, Charles A. and Mary R. Beard, *The Rise of American Civilization,* 2 vols. (New York, 1927); Howard K. Beale, "The Tariff and Reconstruction," *American Historical Review,* XXXV (1930), pp. 276–94; Beale, *The Critical Year,* cited above; Matthew Josephson, *The Politicos* (New York, 1938); and Louis M. Hacker, *The Triumph of American Capitalism* (New York, 1940). Henry L. Swint, "Northern Interest in the Shoeless Southerner," *Journal of Southern History,* XVI (1950), pp. 457–71, suggests that northern humanitarians were partially motivated by economic self-interest. But several recent studies demonstrate convincingly the inadequacy of a simple economic interpretation of reconstruction: Stanley Cohen, "Northeastern Business and Radical Reconstruction: A Re-examination," *Mississippi Valley Historical Review,* XLVI (1959), pp. 67–90; Robert P. Sharkey, *Money, Class, and Party: An Economic Study of Civil War and Reconstruction* (Baltimore, 1959); and Irwin Unger, *The Greenback Era: A Social and Political History of American Finance, 1865–1879* (Princeton, 1964).

Both Cox, *Politics, Principle, and Prejudice,* and Brock, *An American Crisis,* cited above, take seriously the radicals' professions of idealistic motives for their advocacy of civil and political rights for southern Negroes. For the role of the abolitionists in reconstruction see James M. McPherson, *The Struggle for Equality: Abolitionists and the Negro in the Civil War and Reconstruction* (Princeton, 1964). Other works that stress the high principles of the radicals include Ralph Korngold, *Thaddeus Stevens: A Being Darkly Wise and Rudely Great* (New York, 1955); Irving H. Bartlett, *Wendell Phillips: Brahmin Radical* (Boston, 1961); Benjamin P. Thomas and Harold M. Hyman, *Stanton: The Life and Times of Lincoln's Secre-*

tary of War (New York, 1962); Hans L. Trefouse, *Benjamin F. Wade, Radical Republican from Ohio* (New York, 1963); David Montgomery, "Radical Republicanism in Pennsylvania, 1866–1873," *Pennsylvania Magazine of History and Biography*, LXXXV (1961), pp. 439–57; and Ira V. Brown, "Pennsylvania and the Rights of the Negro, 1865–1887," *Pennsylvania History*, XXVIII (1961), pp. 45–57. For a study of one of the influential religious groups supporting the radicals, see Ralph Morrow, *Northern Methodism and Reconstruction* (East Lansing, 1956).

The books by McKitrick, Cox, and Brock, cited above, are excellent for the development of the Republican reconstruction program. For the issue of land reform, see Paul W. Gates, "Federal Land Policy in the South, 1866–1888," *Journal of Southern History*, VI (1940), pp. 303–30; John G. Sproat, "Blueprint for Radical Reconstruction," *Journal of Southern History*, XXIII (1957), pp. 25–44; LaWanda Cox, "The Promise of Land for the Freedman," *Mississippi Valley Historical Review*, XLV (1958), pp. 413–40; Fawn M. Brodie, *Thaddeus Stevens: Scourge of the South* (New York, 1959); and Willie Lee Rose, *Rehearsal for Reconstruction: The Port Royal Experiment* (Indianapolis, 1964). For the Republican obsession with oaths as a test of loyalty, see Harold M. Hyman, *Era of the Oath* (Philadelphia, 1954).

Joseph B. James, *The Framing of the Fourteenth Amendment* (Urbana, Ill., 1956), is the best general work on the subject. The economic interpretation of the Fourteenth Amendment is refuted in Louis B. Boudin, "Truth and Fiction about the Fourteenth Amendment," *New York University Law Review*, XVI (1938), pp. 19–82; Howard J. Graham, "The 'Conspiracy Theory' of the Fourteenth Amendment," *Yale Law Review*, XLVII (1938), pp. 371–403, XLVIII (1938), pp. 171–94; and

James F. S. Russell, "The Railroads in the 'Conspiracy Theory' of the Fourteenth Amendment," *Mississippi Valley Historical Review,* XLI (1955), pp. 601–22. The relationship of the amendment to the aims of the abolitionists is developed in Howard J. Graham, "The Early Antislavery Backgrounds of the Fourteenth Amendment," *Wisconsin Law Review* (1950), pp. 479–507, 610–61; John P. Frank and Robert Munro, "The Original Understanding of 'Equal Protection of the Laws,' " *Columbia Law Review,* L (1950), pp. 131–69; and Jacobus tenBroek, *The Antislavery Origins of the Fourteenth Amendment* (Berkeley, 1951). For the early debate on the relevance of the amendment to social segregation, see Howard J. Graham, "The Fourteenth Amendment and School Segregation," *Buffalo Law Review,* III (1953), pp. 1–24; Alexander M. Bickel, "The Original Understanding and the Segregation Decision," *Harvard Law Review,* LXIX (1955), pp. 1–65; Alfred H. Kelly, "The Congressional Controversy over School Segregation, 1867–1875," *American Historical Review,* LXIV (1959), pp. 537–63; Robert J. Harris, *The Quest for Equality* (Baton Rouge, 1960).

Everette Swinney, "Enforcing the Fifteenth Amendment, 1870–1877," *Journal of Southern History,* XXVIII (1962), pp. 202–18, demonstrates the need for the Force Acts and explains why ultimately they were not effective.

All of Johnson's biographers deal extensively with his impeachment, and all come to his defense. See also McKitrick, *Andrew Johnson and Reconstruction,* cited above; David M. DeWitt, *The Impeachment and Trial of Andrew Johnson* (New York, 1903); David Donald, "Why They Impeached Andrew Johnson," *American Heritage,* VIII (1956), pp. 21–5, 102–3; Ralph J. Roske, "The Seven Martyrs?" *American Historical Review,* LXIV (1959), pp. 323–30; and Harold M. Hyman, "Johnson, Stanton, and

Grant: A Reconsideration of the Army's Role in the Events Leading to Impeachment," *American Historical Review,* LXVI (1960), pp. 85–100.

George R. Bentley, *A History of the Freedmen's Bureau* (Philadelphia, 1955), is a fair and scholarly study of that controversial federal agency. See also Weymouth T. Jordan, "The Freedmen's Bureau in Tennessee," *East Tennessee Historical Society Publications,* No. 11 (1939), pp. 47–61; John C. Engelsman, "The Freedmen's Bureau in Louisiana," *Louisiana Historical Quarterly,* XXXII (1949), pp. 145–224; Elizabeth Bethel, "The Freedmen's Bureau in Alabama," *Journal of Southern History,* XIV (1948), pp. 49–92; William T. Alderson, Jr., "The Freedmen's Bureau and Negro Education in Virginia," *North Carolina Historical Review,* XXIX (1952), pp. 64–90; Claude Elliott, "The Freedmen's Bureau in Texas," *Southwest Historical Quarterly,* LVI (1952), pp. 1–24; Martin Abbott, "The Freedmen's Bureau and Negro Schooling in South Carolina," *South Carolina Historical Magazine,* LVII (1956), pp. 65–81; John and LaWanda Cox, "General O. O. Howard and the 'Misrepresented Bureau,' " *Journal of Southern History,* XIX (1953), pp. 427–56; Martin Abbott, "Free Land, Free Labor, and the Freedmen's Bureau," *Agricultural History,* XXX (1956), pp. 150–7.

Most of the studies of reconstruction in the individual states were written by scholars influenced by Dunning. Though anti-Negro and anti-radical, most of them have not yet been superseded and remain valuable for factual detail. The following Dunning-school studies must still be consulted: Hamilton J. Eckenrode, *The Political History of Virginia during the Reconstruction* (Baltimore, 1904); J. G. de Roulhac Hamilton, *Reconstruction in North Carolina* (New York, 1914); C. Mildred Thompson, *Recon-*

struction in Georgia (New York, 1915); William˙ W.
Davis, *The Civil War and Reconstruction in Florida*
(New York, 1913); Walter L. Fleming, *Civil War and Re-
construction in Alabama* (New York, 1905); James W.
Garner, *Reconstruction in Mississippi* (New York, 1901);
John R. Ficklen, *History of Reconstruction in Louisiana
(through 1868)* (Baltimore, 1910); Ella Lonn, *Reconstruc-
tion in Louisiana after 1868* (New York, 1918); Thomas
S. Staples, *Reconstruction in Arkansas* (New York, 1923);
Charles W. Ramsdell, *Reconstruction in Texas* (New
York, 1910); and W. C. Nunn, *Texas under the Carpet-
baggers* (Austin, 1962).

For revisionist studies of individual states, see Thomas
B. Alexander, *Political Reconstruction in Tennessee*
(Nashville, 1950); Francis B. Simkins and Robert H.
Woody, *South Carolina during Reconstruction* (Chapel
Hill, 1932); Horace M. Bond, "Social and Economic
Forces in Alabama Reconstruction," *Journal of Negro
History*, XXIII (1938), pp. 290–348; Thomas B. Alexan-
der, "Persistent Whiggery in Alabama and the Lower
South, 1860–1867," *Alabama Review*, XII (1959), pp. 35–
52; Roger W. Shugg, *Origins of Class Struggle in Louisi-
ana* (Baton Rouge, 1939); T. Harry Williams, "The
Louisiana Reunification Movement of 1873," *Journal of
Southern History*, XI (1945), pp. 349–69; Willie M.
Caskey, *Secession and Restoration of Louisiana* (Baton
Rouge, 1938).

A good general study of the role of the Negro in reconstruction remains to be written. Henderson H. Donald,
The Negro Freedman (New York, 1952), the only study
now available, does not fill this need but should be consulted. Three valuable books deal with special aspects of
this topic: Paul Lewinson, *Race, Class, and Party: A History of Negro Suffrage and White Politics in the South*,

(New York, 1932); Samuel D. Smith, *The Negro in Congress, 1870–1901* (Chapel Hill, 1940); and Otis Singletary, *Negro Militia and Reconstruction* (Austin, 1957). Alrutheus A. Taylor describes the role of the Negro in three southern states: *The Negro in South Carolina during the Reconstruction* (Washington, D.C., 1924); *The Negro in the Reconstruction of Virginia* (Washington, D.C., 1926); and *The Negro in Tennessee, 1865–1880* (Washington, D.C., 1941). Joel R. Williamson has written an excellent new study of the Negro in the reconstruction of South Carolina, soon to be published by the University of North Carolina Press. Vernon Lane Wharton, *The Negro in Mississippi, 1865–1890* (Chapel Hill, 1947), a model monograph, is one of the most important revisionist studies that has yet been published. The extent to which I have used it is only partially acknowledged in my footnotes.

All the state studies deal extensively with the carpetbaggers and scalawags, but detailed monographs about both groups are needed. Four interpretive articles are especially valuable: Richard N. Current, "Carpetbaggers Reconsidered," in *A Festschrift for Frederick B. Artz* (Durham, 1964), pp. 139–57; David Donald, "The Scalawag in Mississippi Reconstruction," *Journal of Southern History*, X (1944), pp. 447–60; Thomas B. Alexander, "Persistent Whiggery in the Confederate South, 1860–1877," *Journal of Southern History*, XXVII (1961), pp. 305–29; and Allen W. Trelease, "Who Were the Scalawags?" *Journal of Southern History*, XXIX (1963), pp. 445–68. See also Henry L. Swint, *The Northern Teacher in the South, 1862–1870* (Nashville, 1941); and Jonathan Daniels, *Prince of Carpetbaggers* (Philadelphia, 1958).

Jack B. Scroggs stresses the positive achievements of the southern radical regimes in two revisionist articles: "Southern Reconstruction: A Radical View," *Journal of Southern History*, XXIV (1958), pp. 407–29; and "Carpetbagger Constitutional Reform in the South Atlantic States, 1867–1868," *Journal of Southern History,* XXVII (1961), pp. 475–93. For a study of the first significant experiment in integrated education in the South, see Louis R. Harlan, "Desegregation in New Orleans Public Schools during Reconstruction," *American Historical Review,* LXVII (1962), pp. 663–75. The financial policies of the radical governments are discussed in George L. Anderson, "The South and Problems of Post-Civil War Finance," *Journal of Southern History,* IX (1943), pp. 181–95; Carter Goodrich, "Public Aid to Railroads in the Reconstruction South," *Political Science Quarterly,* LXXI (1956), pp. 407–42; and John F. Stover, *The Railroads of the South, 1865–1900: A Study of Finance and Control* (Chapel Hill, 1955). The issue of the disenfranchisement of ex-Confederates is treated in William A. Russ, Jr., "Registration and Disfranchisement under Radical Reconstruction," *Mississippi Valley Historical Review,* XXI (1934), pp. 163–80.

For the social, political, and economic forces that caused Northerners to react against radical reconstruction, see Earle D. Ross, *The Liberal Republican Movement* (New York, 1919); William B. Hesseltine, *Ulysses S. Grant, Politician* (New York, 1935); William B. Hesseltine, "Economic Factors in the Abandonment of Reconstruction," *Mississippi Valley Historical Review,* XXII (1935), pp. 191–210; Paul H. Buck, *The Road to Reunion* (Boston, 1937); Patrick W. Riddleberger, "The Break in the Radical Ranks: Liberals vs Stalwarts in the Election of 1872," *Journal of Negro History,* XLIV (1959), pp. 136–57; Patrick W. Riddleberger, "The Radicals' Abandonment of the Negro during Reconstruction," *Journal of Negro History,* XLV (1960), pp. 88–102; and Richard B. Drake, "Freedman's Aid Societies and Sectional Compromise," *Journal of Southern History,* XXIX (1963), pp. 175–86.

All of the state studies deal with the overthrow of the

radical regimes. See also Stanley F. Horn, *Invisible Empire: The Story of the Ku Klux Klan, 1866–1871* (Boston, 1939); Francis B. Simkins, "The Ku Klux Klan in South Carolina," *Journal of Negro History,* XII (1927), pp. 606–47; Grady McWhiney and Francis B. Simkins, "The Ghostly Legend of the Ku-Klux Klan," *Negro History Bulletin,* XIV (1951), pp. 109–12; Alfred B. Williams, *Hampton and His Red Shirts* (Charleston, 1935); Garnie W. McGinty, *Louisiana Redeemed: The Overthrow of the Carpetbag Rule, 1876–1880* (New Orleans, 1941); and Wharton, *The Negro in Mississippi,* cited above.

An old but still useful study of the election of 1876 is Paul L. Haworth, *The Hayes-Tilden Disputed Presidential Election of 1876* (Cleveland, 1906). On the Compromise of 1877, it has been superseded by C. Vann Woodward, *Reunion and Reaction: The Compromise of 1877 and the End of Reconstruction* (Boston, 1951).

In addition to the works cited above, my book is based on research in relevant government documents, contemporary periodicals, and the published diaries, letters, and memoirs of numerous participants in reconstruction politics. I have consulted the papers of Carl Schurz, John Sherman, and Thaddeus Stevens in the Library of Congress; of Oliver P. Morton in the Indiana State Library, Indianapolis; and of Zachariah Chandler, George W. Julian, Abraham Lincoln, Lyman Trumbull, and Benjamin F. Wade on microfilm in the University of California Library, Berkeley.

Four printed collections of sources are available to interested readers: Edward McPherson, ed., *The Political History of the United States of America during the Period of Reconstruction* (Washington, D.C., 1875), a collection of public documents; Walter L. Fleming, ed., *Documentary History of Reconstruction,* 2 vols. (Cleveland, 1906–1907), a large collection but weighted against the radicals; Benjamin B. Kendrick, ed., *The Journal of the Joint Committee of Fifteen on Reconstruction* (New York, 1914); and James P. Shenton, ed., *The Reconstruction: A Documentary History of the South after the War, 1865–1877* (New York, 1963), a well-chosen brief collection.

INDEX

Index

Index

A NOTE ABOUT THE AUTHOR

KENNETH M. STAMPP is Professor of American History at the University of California (Berkeley). A native of Milwaukee, he earned his B.A., M.A., and Ph.D. degrees at the University of Wisconsin. He taught at the universities of Wisconsin, Arkansas, and Maryland before his appointment at Berkeley in 1946. While at Wisconsin, he was a President Adams Fellow in History, and he was a John Simon Guggenheim Fellow in 1952–3.

A specialist in Civil War history, Mr. Stampp is the author of *Indiana Politics during the Civil War, And the War Came,* and *The Peculiar Institution* (available in Vintage Books) . He edited *The Causes of the Civil War* (1959) and was co-author of *The American Experience* (1963).

VINTAGE POLITICAL SCIENCE
AND SOCIAL CRITICISM

A free catalogue of VINTAGE BOOKS *will be sent at your request. Write to* Vintage Books, 457 Madison Avenue, New York, New York 10022.

VINTAGE HISTORY—AMERICAN

VINTAGE HISTORY AND CRITICISM OF
LITERATURE, MUSIC, AND ART

A free catalogue of VINTAGE BOOKS *will be sent at your request. Write to* Vintage Books, 457 Madison Avenue, New York, New York 10022.

A SELECT LIST OF
VINTAGE RUSSIAN LIBRARY

A free catalogue of VINTAGE BOOKS *will be sent at your request. Write to* Vintage Books, 457 Madison Avenue, New York, New York 10022.